THE DAUGHTER I HAD TO BE

An Inner Awakening Through Shadow Work and Divine Feminine Healing

Emily Elizabeth Hickman

Title: THE DAUGHTER I HAD TO BE
Author: Emily Elizabeth Hickman
Copyright ©2026 by Emily Elizabeth Hickman
All rights reserved.
No part of this book may be reproduced, distributed, or transmitted in any form or by any means, including photocopying, recording, or other electronic or mechanical methods, without the prior written permission of the publisher, except in the case of brief quotations embodied in critical reviews and certain other noncommercial uses permitted by copyright law. For permission requests, write to the publisher at the address below.
Published by Pine Tree Press

www.pinetreepress.com

Printed in USA

This book is dedicated to my children.
You will never know how many times you saved my life.

TABLE OF CONTENTS

ACKNOWLEDGMENTS

This book was written during seasons of growth, reflection, and healing. I am deeply grateful to the people who supported me along the way.

To my children, thank you for being my reason to keep moving forward and for reminding me, again and again, why healing matters. You have shaped not only who I am as a mother, but who I am as a person.

To the mountains of eastern Kentucky, where I was born and raised, thank you for grounding me in resilience, strength, and quiet perseverance.

To the individuals I have worked with throughout my career, thank you for trusting me with your stories. Your courage, vulnerability, and resilience have deeply shaped my understanding of healing and human connection.

To the friends, mentors, and loved ones who supported me through difficult seasons, thank you for your patience, encouragement, and belief in me, even when I struggled to believe in myself.

And finally, to the readers, those who see parts of themselves in these pages, thank you for being here. This book was written with you in mind.

Chapter 1:

WHAT IS SHADOW WORK?

"The light you're looking for is hidden in the dark."

The Light Hidden in the Dark

There comes a moment—maybe after years of holding it together, or maybe just in the middle of an ordinary day—when something inside you shifts.

You stop asking, "What's wrong with me?" and you start asking, "What happened to me?"

That moment is everything. It's sacred, even if it doesn't feel that way.

Even if you're crying on the bathroom floor or sitting in your car staring at the steering wheel, too numb to move.

It's the split second where the mask cracks and the truth begins to breathe.

It is where survival stops feeling like strength and starts to feel like a weight you can't carry one more step.

Shadow work begins in that space— the messy, unfiltered, unapologetic middle ground where the self you've hidden collides with the self you pretend to be.

Not in some perfect spiritual retreat or glowing sunrise epiphany, but right there, where the life you've been performing starts to crumble.

It's not tidy or cute. It's definitely not the kind of thing you post with angel numbers and dreamy filters. It's raw. Uncomfortable. Sometimes ugly, but it's honest and it's yours.

Shadow work is about getting real with the parts of yourself you were told weren't okay to have.

The anger you shoved down. The sadness you hid because it made other people uncomfortable. They want you silenced to feel loved.

The *you* that got buried under years of survival. This isn't about fixing yourself. You're not broken.

It's about slowly, gently reclaiming the parts of you that you disowned.

It's about reclaiming those pieces, piece by piece, until we feel whole again— not perfect, but whole.

You don't have to feel "ready." You don't have to be spiritual or know all the right terms or believe in anything but the small whisper inside you that says,

There's more to me than this.

All you need is curiosity.

A little willingness to turn inward.

To pause.

To ask better questions.

That's it.

That's where we begin.

Far from Finished

I'd heard the term "shadow work" long before I truly understood it. It showed up in podcasts, therapy circles, and in my master's program in counseling. I studied Jung. I could talk about archetypes and the unconscious. I knew how to guide people to the "root cause" of their issues. I helped others untangle their emotional knots. I believed I'd done mine—at least enough to keep going.

After all, I'd survived so much already. I was the one who rose, no matter how many times life tried to break me. I had built a life, a career, a sense of identity around helping others heal. On the outside, it probably looked like I had made it through the fire despite the odds. But survival isn't the same as healing. Not even close.

You can go a long time thinking you're fine. You can function, perform, even thrive in ways that look impressive. You can tell yourself you've already dealt with the past. Maybe you've even made some peace with it—or at least tucked it away neatly enough to keep moving. But then life hits harder than you're prepared for. It doesn't knock politely—it crashes through everything.

That's when the shadow rises. That's when the truth starts speaking louder than your coping mechanisms. For me, it wasn't one thing—it was all of it, all at once. Another divorce. The quiet, painful realization that I was using alcohol to cope. A complicated relationship with a man much younger than me, who reflected back every part of me I didn't want to see.

The Beginning of Everything

The long, isolating months of COVID. The depression felt like it had no bottom. My daughter, unraveling in her own storm of teenage pain. My son, stepping into the vulnerable, unsteady world of adolescence. And then—my mother. Cutting me off. Again. Just like she had when I was thirteen.

But this time, my grandmother, the woman who had truly raised me, was gone. My last tether to feeling unconditionally loved. Her loss hit like an earthquake, ripping up the foundations I thought I had built. Suddenly, I couldn't outrun anything anymore.

The titles, the roles, the stories I'd used to hold myself together—they all started to fall away. The woman who could always roll with the punches was gone. She was buried beneath years of pain she had never been allowed to feel.

That's when the real work began. Not the intellectual work. Not the checklists or the healing journals or the morning rituals. I'm talking about the kind of shadow work that cracks you open—not to punish you, but to finally show you who you really are underneath all the armor.

This wasn't something I chose out of curiosity. It was a necessity. Because I refused to be swallowed by the dark. Not for me. For my daughter, who needed to see what it looked like to truly live, even after the worst of it. She needed to see that you can come back from it. That you can fall apart and still choose to rise, not in spite of the darkness, but because you finally stopped running from it.

That was the moment I stopped trying to "get back to myself." The truth is, I had never really met her. Not fully. Not until everything I used to be fell away, and I was left standing face-to-face with the woman underneath it all.

That was the beginning of everything.

How the Shadow Is Formed

The shadow doesn't appear all at once. It doesn't crash in like a storm—it gathers slowly, quietly, over time. It forms in the pauses between what we need and what we receive. In the silences where we should have been comforted. In the moments when our truth was too much, our feelings too loud, our needs too inconvenient.

It begins when we're too young to make sense of it all—too small to name what we're feeling, yet just aware enough to notice that some parts of us are not welcome. For me, it began in childhood. Not through loud explosions of trauma, although there were many of those. But through the subtle, constant rewiring of who I was allowed to be.

I learned early that my needs came second. Or not at all. That being helpful was more appreciated than being honest. That keeping the peace mattered more than being seen. I was always watching. Especially my mother—her moods were the weather, and I adjusted accordingly. Her silence could fill a room like thunder. Without a word, I learned to scan her face before I spoke, to shape-shift into whatever might keep her calm—or at least keep her from turning away.

It didn't take long before I stopped asking myself what I needed, and started asking what might keep her okay. When the emotional weight got too heavy, I didn't fall apart—I adapted. I became who I thought I needed to be. The caretaker. The emotional translator. The one who didn't ask for much. The one who always knew how to make things easier for everyone else.

I wore that mask so well, even I started to believe it was me. That's how the shadow forms. Not always through big, dramatic moments—but through the quiet, repeated conditioning of self-abandonment. When you're constantly shown—directly or indirectly—that your emotions are a burden, that your boundaries are optional, that your truth makes things harder... You don't just let those parts of yourself go. You bury them. You push them deep down, hoping it will make you more lovable. More accepted. Less of a problem.

But buried doesn't mean gone. It means hidden. Forgotten. Repressed. Pushed into the dark corners of your psyche where you think they can't hurt you—or anyone else—anymore. But they don't disappear. All of it—your anger, your fear, your grief, your longing, your joy, your boundaries, your wildness—it doesn't die just because you learned to survive without it.

It waits. Those exiled parts of you wait in the dark for the moment when you're no longer surviving day to day—when you're strong enough, safe enough, ready enough to go looking for them. To reclaim them. To say: *You were never too much. You were just too much for someone who didn't know how to love all of you.*

That's when the real healing begins. Not by becoming someone new, but by slowly, bravely returning to who you were before the world taught you to hide.

Why We Resist Shadow Work

No one teaches you how to understand your emotions in a world that rewards you for pretending everything is fine. We don't avoid shadow work because we are lazy or don't care. We avoid it because we have been trained to. We learn that talking about our dark feelings makes others uncomfortable. That sadness is weakness. That polite smiles are safer than honest truths.

Even as a little girl, I carried a weight I couldn't name. I didn't know where it came from—only that it was always there, like a slow, steady hum beneath every happy moment. Looking back, I realize I was too busy to feel. The pain was there, but it was wrapped in silence, numbed with movement. I wasn't taught to understand myself—I was taught to push forward.

To be the "good one." The quiet one. The non-disruptive one. The one who doesn't cause a scene, even when her soul is collapsing. That is why so many resist shadow work—it threatens the version of themselves they've been praised for—the high-functioning one, the overachiever, the survivor, the "strong one."

What Shadow Work Offers

Shadow work isn't about fixing yourself—it's about remembering yourself. It's a quiet invitation to look beneath all the roles you've taken on and ask, with gentle honesty, "*Why do I do what I do? Who am I beneath the habits and expectations? What might life feel like if I stopped operating on autopilot and truly came home to myself?*"

This work isn't about perfection or constant transformation. It's about turning inward and making space for what's been buried: your truth, your wounds, your wisdom, and allowing yourself to be authentic, not just functional.

The beauty of shadow work is that it doesn't just serve you; it changes the way you show up in the world. It softens the edges you once thought you needed to survive. It expands your compassion and clarity. It helps you break generational cycles you didn't even know you were caught in.

When you begin to see and hold your own pain with tenderness, you stop unconsciously passing it on. You stop needing other people to carry what was never theirs to hold. That healing ripples into your relationships, your parenting, your boundaries, and your ability to sit with others without needing to fix them—or yourself.

This path isn't just for the spiritual or the broken; it's for overachievers and caretakers, those who feel they belong everywhere and nowhere. It's for those who smile through tired eyes, follow and break rules in search of something real, and struggle with stillness because it forces them to confront the unnameable.

Anyone can carry shadows, and anyone can begin to heal them, regardless of their story. Some shadows are darker than others, shaped by trauma, grief, betrayal, or pain passed down like heirlooms. But none of them are beyond healing. Every shadow is a part of you that once served a purpose, even if that purpose was simply to help you survive.

These parts don't need to be erased. They need to be met with presence, not punishment. Every human being deserves to be seen and held in their wholeness, not just in their strength or their successes. We all need at least one person who can sit with us in the dark without trying to pull us into the light too quickly. That kind of presence is medicine. That kind of love cracks the armor.

That's what shadow work truly offers: a path back to that kind of presence within yourself. When you learn to offer your own shadow compassion instead of judgment, when you stop needing to be "fixed" and start allowing yourself to be felt, you reclaim something sacred. You find peace not by changing the world, but by making peace with yourself, including your darkness.

When that happens, something powerful shifts. You begin to walk through the world differently. Softer. Freer. Braver. And maybe, without even realizing it, you give someone else permission to do the same.

Getting Started

Shadow work doesn't begin with a perfectly highlighted journal, a spiritual checklist, or a clear plan. It begins with something much quieter: permission. Permission to feel what you've been pushing down for years. Permission to stop running from the parts of yourself that feel heavy or complicated. Permission to sit with what hurts without rushing to fix it.

That's where the real work starts. It's not about doing it "right." It's about allowing yourself to begin from wherever you are, messy emotions and all. And for many of us, that first step doesn't come through structure or formulas—it comes through releasing our pain in ways that don't destroy us.

Maybe for you it won't be journaling. Maybe it's music, or art, or a long walk in silence. Maybe it's talking with a friend, crying in the shower, dancing in your bedroom with your eyes closed, or screaming into a pillow when the pressure finally becomes too much. Maybe it's as simple as placing a hand on your heart and saying, *"I'm still here."*

For me, it began with a pen. Not because I was ready, but because I had tried everything else. I used to reach for liquor to numb the pain, to quiet the noise in my head until I couldn't feel anything at all. But eventually, I picked up a different kind of bottle—ink and let it spill across the page. I started writing poems. Some were angry. Some were deeply sad.

Others made me laugh with how absurd and honest they were. I wasn't trying to be a writer. I wasn't trying to be profound. I was just trying to survive in a way that felt less like self-destruction and more like self-return.

What surprised me most was that, somewhere in the mess of those poems, I found my voice again—the voice I didn't realize I had lost so long ago. When I was twelve, I learned that my voice could be dangerous. I had written in my journal about a first kiss, something small and innocent. My mother found it, read it out loud to our extended family, and used my words as a way to shame me.

That moment pierced something in me. Surrounded by people who were supposed to protect me, I felt exposed and humiliated. And I shut down. After that, I didn't write honestly. Even in college, I avoided journaling, even when it was assigned. And to this day, when I pick up a pen, there are moments when I still feel the echo of that experience—the whisper in my mind saying, *"Don't tell the truth. It's not safe."*

That voice is part of my shadow. Shadow work is the moment I turn toward it and say, "I see you. I know where you came from. But I'm not letting you decide how I live anymore."

The shadow isn't just the pain or trauma itself. It's the strategy you built around that pain to survive. For me, writing became one of the most powerful ways to peel back those layers. Not through perfectly structured prompts or forced insights, but by simply letting the words come as they were. No expectations. No editing. Just a safe space to witness what was already inside me, waiting to be heard.

If you don't know where to begin, start small. Let your thoughts lead. You don't need to write anything beautiful or even coherent. Just put down the first thing that comes to mind, and then the next. Follow the thread, even if it doesn't make sense yet. Talk to yourself like you would a scared child—with patience, with curiosity, with love.

When something stings or brings up resistance, pause and ask, *"When did I first feel this way? What part of me stopped being safe to show?"* Even the things you avoid—like writing, dancing, resting—might be clues. Often, resistance is just a part of you asking to be seen, not avoided.

And please, don't try to do all of this alone.

If you're lucky, you'll find someone who can sit with you through the unraveling. For me, that person was my cousin. We shared poetry. We cried together over our mothers. We laughed through the pain, sometimes in the same breath. She didn't offer advice or try to fix me. She simply held space, loved me anyway, and showed up. That saved me more than she will ever fully understand.

Shadow work begins within, but it deepens in connection. We're not meant to heal in isolation. If you haven't found that safe person yet, I hope you do. Even more than that, I hope you become that kind of person—for yourself, and for someone else.

We all need someone in our lives who can hold space for us without trying to fix us. Someone who doesn't flinch at our pain or rush us out of our grief. That kind of presence is rare, but it's life-changing. And the beautiful thing is, shadow work helps you become that person for yourself.

It teaches you how to sit with your own discomfort instead of running from it. It helps you meet yourself with honesty instead of shame. And when you do that, something begins to shift. You stop projecting your pain onto others. You stop needing the world around you to adjust just so you can feel okay. You start to feel steady within yourself, not because everything is perfect, but because you're no longer abandoning the parts of you that hurt.

This kind of healing doesn't happen overnight. It's not flashy or linear. It's quiet, gradual, and deeply personal. But as you begin to turn toward yourself with more gentleness, you create space for something sacred. You begin to feel more complete, more honest, and freer.

And maybe, without even trying, you become the safe place someone else has been longing to find. When we learn how to hold space for our own darkness, we naturally become the kind of light that helps others face theirs. Not by pulling them out, but by showing them they don't have to be afraid to go in.

Coming Home to Yourself

You don't have to figure everything out today. You don't have to have a five-step plan or a perfectly outlined healing journey. You just have to begin. That's it. Just take one honest breath, one quiet pause, one moment where you allow yourself to say, *"I want something different. I want to feel more like myself again."*

Shadow work isn't about diving headfirst into all the pain at once. It's not about ripping yourself open or forcing breakthroughs before you're ready. It's about lighting one small candle at a time. One small moment of truth. One flicker of curiosity that says, *"What's hiding underneath this part of me?"*

You follow that soft glow, gently and slowly, into the places where you first learned to tuck parts of yourself away in order to be accepted, safe, or loved. In the next chapter, we're going to explore those early moments. The ones that don't always seem dramatic from the outside, but live quietly inside you, shaping how you show up in the world.

These are the moments that taught you how to adapt instead of express. How to keep the peace instead of speaking your truth. How to read the room before you ever learned to read a book. Somewhere along the way, you began to shape-shift to become who others needed you to be. And while that protected you at the time, it also came at a cost.

The cost was often your own voice, your own needs, your own sense of self. Together, we'll begin the gentle, steady work of untangling those patterns. Not with blame or harshness, but with compassion. Because healing doesn't come from forcing yourself to be someone new. It comes from remembering.

It comes from turning toward the younger version of you, the one who started hiding, the one who made herself small, the one who did what she had to do to survive, and saying, *"I see you. You did the best you could. But we don't have to live this way anymore."*

You're not broken. You're not too far gone. You're just waiting to come back home to yourself. And I promise that journey is worth it.

Shadow Sheets

1. Who Are You, Really? If you could describe yourself in a few words, what would they be? Do you think others would describe you the same way?

----

2. Hidden Strengths: What are some things you're naturally good at or that come easily to you, even if you don't always give yourself credit for them?

----

3. Forgotten Joys: Are there activities you loved as a child that you don't make time for anymore?

----

4. Secret Talents: Is there a side of yourself that you don't share often, but that you secretly enjoy?

Checking In with Yourself:

5. Small Sparks: What kinds of things make you feel excited, curious, or alive, even in small moments?

----

6. Unexpected Strengths: Have you ever surprised yourself by handling a tough situation better than you expected?

Starting to Reflect:

7. Hidden Gifts: Are there qualities or strengths you've been told to tone down or hide?

----

8. Your Unique Perspective: What's something you see differently than most people, and how has that shaped who you are?

----

9. Quiet Confidence: What's something you know about yourself that you don't often share, but that makes you proud?

Setting the Tone for Growth:

10. Getting Curious: What's one small way you could let a hidden part of yourself shine a little more this week?

Chapter 2:

ADAPTIVE, NOT AUTHENTIC

"Generational trauma, unnamed wounds, and the legacy of denial."

Who I Had to Become

When I look back, I realize I became someone else long before I even knew who I was. I adapted, not because I wanted to, but because I was being trained to. I didn't become myself. I became who I had to be. That becoming didn't happen in a single moment. It happened gradually, silently—the way fog rolls in without warning. One day, you can see the edges of your reflection clearly, and the next, you're shape-shifting in the name of survival.

I didn't grow into who I was. I adapted to the roles that earned me safety, praise, or simply less chaos. I didn't make a conscious decision to betray myself, I was just becoming. Like all children, I was learning the rules—the silent agreements that shape our place in the world before we're old enough to question them.

I learned what could be spoken and what had to be swallowed. I learned which feelings made people uncomfortable and which ones earned me approval. I knew that being helpful, quiet, or uncomplicated got me love. I also learned that asking for too much, crying too hard, or simply taking up emotional space could turn the room cold. Without ever being told directly, I was being trained to stay emotionally small.

In families where pain is unspoken or pushed aside, the silence becomes its own kind of language. When you grow up in a divided home, you start to recognize the unspoken boundaries that stretch far beyond physical walls. Some truths feel dangerous to speak, and some emotions feel like landmines. You're taught that what happens with one parent stays with that parent. You learn not to say too much, not to connect dots that others work hard to keep separated.

So you split yourself instead. You become one version of yourself in one home and another version in the other. Maybe at school or with friends, you're someone else entirely. Eventually, it starts to feel normal.

Over time, this kind of adaptation can start to feel like love. You think you're being accepted, but what's really being welcomed is the version of you that knows how to manage everyone else's comfort. You learn to read the room before you know how to read your own emotions. You start to believe that shrinking your true self is what keeps you close to people. That blending in is the same as belonging. That saying nothing is better than being misunderstood.

Adaptation is a clever kind of betrayal. You don't mean to abandon yourself. It just happens so gradually that you don't even realize you've done it. It's a subtle kind of loss. A disconnection that looks like maturity from the outside. You become dependable. Low-maintenance. Easy to be around. But you also stop being able to hear your own voice.

Eventually, you start to feel like a stranger in your own skin. You don't know what you really want, only what others expect. You don't know what you really feel, only what you're allowed to express. Somewhere inside, you start to believe that maybe your real self wasn't good enough after all. Too emotional. Too sensitive. Too complicated.

But none of that is true.

The truth is, silence is not safety. It's a slow kind of suffocation. Being small might keep the peace for a while, but it also keeps you from being fully alive. At some point, the weight of everything you've swallowed becomes too heavy to carry alone. The cost of staying hidden, of splitting yourself to survive, is steep.

But you don't have to stay there. You don't have to keep abandoning who you are just to be accepted by people who only know the version of you that fits their comfort. You can come back to yourself, even if it feels unfamiliar at first.

Healing begins when you stop asking who others need you to be and start asking who you were before you ever learned to perform.

I don't remember ever deciding to be quiet, but somewhere in early childhood, I learned that my silence was appreciated. That my withdrawal was rewarded. In preschool and early elementary school, my teachers told my mother I was *"too shy, too quiet, too withdrawn."* They said I needed to *"come out of my shell."*

I didn't feel shy. I felt unattached. At recess, I hid in the concrete tunnel on the playground, letting the echo of my own thoughts muffle the noise around me. I wasn't drawn to the chaos of games or the swirl of friendships. I didn't understand the alliances and betrayals that played out. I didn't want to be with the other kids. I felt rootless, disconnected, and adrift in my own skin. I just felt alone in a way I couldn't name yet, a kind of loneliness that clung to me even when I was surrounded by people.

I didn't want to be there. I wanted to be anywhere else.

When I moved to a city school, teachers started sitting me next to the disruptive kids. The ones who poked, pinched, whispered threatening things. My mom said it was a compliment that I was a *"good influence,"* but all I heard was: your discomfort doesn't matter, your needs come last.

That's how the training deepened. I learned to accept discomfort without protest. You learn that your own pain is second to someone else's, that your discomfort is a sacrifice you should make without complaint, and that your quietness is a virtue as long as it makes someone else's life easier.

You learn to ignore the pinches, the whispers, the threats, because "good girls" don't make a scene, don't push back, and don't make things harder for the adults who are already struggling.

The Choreography of Quiet

Then came acting camp. My mother hoped it would help me break out of my shell. Or maybe she just needed something to fill the time while my brother and cousin went to baseball camp. Either way, she signed me up.

My grandmother drove us over an hour and a half to Knoxville, Tennessee where I learned about singing, stage directions, and the art of pretending convincingly. At the end of camp, I was chosen to sing "Somewhere Over the Rainbow" solo, just me and the piano.

My mom said I did great, but I don't remember it. I only remember the terror of being exposed, of being seen. I remember the lights blinding me, the stage swallowing me whole, my heart pounding so hard I could feel it in my throat. I don't remember the applause, the faces in the audience, or even my own voice. I just remember the fear.

My memory of that moment is a blackout. My brain shut the door on it as if to say: *never again.*

That's when I really learned the art of pretending. I began to polish a version of myself that would never again risk being seen too closely. If being visible meant being that exposed, I wanted no part of it. That's where the art, the survival skill, of acting like everything was fine—of playing a role so no one would ask me if I was drowning—solidified.

That is when I decided that being myself was too painful to be worth it. So I started to play a part. I tried to blend in, to fit in, to act like I wanted to be there, like I was fine, like I wasn't suffocating under the weight of my own unspoken truth. The more I pretended, the more I lost touch with the girl I had been before—the one who didn't need to "come out of her shell" because she had never hidden there in the first place.

That's the Inheritance of Silence—the slow, quiet training that teaches you to bury your truth, to filter your feelings, to sacrifice your authenticity for the comfort of others. It's the mask you wear so well that you forget what your own face looks like.

Silence is a skill, passed down like an art form, learned by daughters who study the expressions their mothers never speak. It's a second language for those of us raised in houses where pain is implied but never confessed—a choreography of quiet.

But silence doesn't always stay quiet.

Generational Trauma

The silence didn't begin with my mother. Just like it didn't begin with me. It's something older, something passed down quietly through generations like an heirloom no one wanted but no one knew how to put down. A wound that lives in the bones of the women who came before me. It shaped the way they moved through the world, the way they loved, the way they hurt. Before I understood it, I was already carrying it too.

My mother's story is the one I know best, but it's only one part of something much larger, a darker thread in a tapestry that stretches farther than any of us can see. Before she became the mother I would spend my life trying to understand, she was just a little girl. She had wide, curious eyes and a soft heart. I like to imagine her that way sometimes—before the pain. But something happened to her. Something that should have broken the silence wide open, but instead sealed it shut.

She was molested as a child, and when she found the courage to tell her mother, my grandmother, the truth was met with silence. Whether out of denial, fear, or her own unresolved trauma, the response was the same: the truth was too dangerous to be spoken.

I don't know exactly what my grandmother said in that moment, or if she said anything at all. But I know that whatever happened in that moment taught my mother to swallow her screams, to choke down her truth, to carry her pain alone. A silent message that some things are too dangerous to be spoken out loud. That telling the truth can cost you love.

Sometimes I picture that moment, I imagine my mother standing in the kitchen, small and trembling, maybe clutching the edge of the counter to steady herself. Her voice barely above a whisper as she tried to say the thing no child should ever have to say. I imagine my grandmother, carrying her own buried history, reacting not from cruelty but from the only survival strategy she had ever known. Look away. Don't feel. Move on.

That was the moment the silence passed from one generation to the next.

But my mother didn't just carry the silence, she shaped herself around it. She learned that if she couldn't speak her truth, she could at least make herself too loud to be ignored. Her voice, once silenced, became sharp. Her pain, once denied, became armor. She didn't just protect herself, she braced herself against the world, ready for it to hurt her again.

Her emotions came in tidal waves, fierce and overwhelming. She lashes out, bites first, and protects herself with the sharp edges of unprocessed rage. Her words are no longer whispers buried in the back of her throat. They are daggers, thrown before anyone else can get close enough to wound her again. Her love came tangled with fear.

Her reactions weren't always fair or safe. She didn't know how to make room for her own pain, so there was never space for mine.

That's how trauma keeps moving. It adapts. It changes form. But it doesn't disappear. Her pain became her shield, her tongue a blade, her presence a storm. What wasn't healed was passed down. What wasn't spoken was absorbed.

Until one day, someone—maybe you, maybe me—decides to stop acting like the silence is normal.

Living with Unnamed Wounds

I didn't know my mother's story when I was a child, but I felt the heaviness in everything. It showed up in the way she pulled back from me when I asked too many questions, the way she tensed when I cried, and how quickly she shut down anything that resembled vulnerability. I felt it in the way she punished me, not always with words, but with withdrawal, silence, or unpredictable outbursts whenever I tried to name what hurt.

At the time, I didn't understand what was happening. I just knew that certain emotions made her uncomfortable and that naming the truth seemed to make things worse, not better. What I see now is that it wasn't just her pain she was trying to bury. She was carrying something older. Something she had inherited. The terror she couldn't speak of as a child had grown into a kind of emotional reflex—deny, deflect, suppress.

Without ever saying it, she passed that reflex on to me. I learned early that some things are better left unsaid, that speaking my truth could make me a target, that the cost of honesty might be isolation or worse—a kind of emotional exile. I learned that silence felt safer than honesty and that certain truths, especially my own, were better kept to myself.

Looking back, I can trace some of the moments when I began to disconnect from myself. Small moments that didn't look like trauma from the outside, but left lasting marks. I remember learning how to hide my real thoughts because they made other people uncomfortable. I learned to swallow my sadness, to smooth over my anger, to offer a smile when all I really wanted was to scream.

I got good at performing. Good at reading the emotional temperature and adjusting myself to make things easier for everyone else. To apologize for my own existence, to shrink to fit a space too small for my real self. Still, there were parts of me that refused to disappear. Somewhere deep down, I knew I wasn't meant to live like this.

When I felt cornered or dismissed, I found other ways to speak. I lashed out. I pushed back. I used sharp words to protect my soft places. I see now that this, too, was a form of adaptation—my mother's unresolved rage echoing through me, teaching me that if I wanted to be heard, I might have to fight for it.

None of this was ever about being dramatic or rebellious. It was about survival. It was about trying to exist in an environment where being honest felt like a risk and where emotional safety was never a given. It was about learning that love sometimes came with conditions and that expression could come at a cost.

It's not always visible to the outside world. It doesn't always leave bruises or scars, but it leaves a mark in other ways. In the way you question your feelings. In the way you police your own voice. In the way you keep people at arm's length, even when all you want is to be close. None of this was rebellion. It was survival.

When emotional safety isn't available, adaptation becomes instinct, and that adaptation, even when it protects you, eventually costs you everything.

The Weight That Came With Me

The silence followed me.

Into adulthood.

Into motherhood.

Into moments where I smiled when I wanted to cry.

Into conversations where I changed the subject instead of speaking the truth.

Into every time I avoided conflict, not because I didn't care, but because I didn't know how to trust my voice.

The Legacy of Denial

This silence didn't just shape my childhood. It followed me into adulthood, like a shadow I couldn't shake. When I became a mother, I started to see the cycle. I repeated the silence. The avoidance. The emotional editing, the same emotional tightrope walking. Not because I wanted to, but because I didn't know another way. I hadn't yet learned how to feel safe with my own emotions, let alone how to model that safety for someone else.

But the thing about silence is that it builds pressure. It becomes a weight, a suffocating force, until one day you can't carry it anymore. One day, the cracks start to show. You find yourself standing in a room full of people, choking on all the words you never said, drowning in the truth you've been taught to deny.

Maybe it happens in a quiet moment. Maybe during an argument. Or maybe when your child asks a question that hits too close to a truth you've been avoiding. For me, it wasn't one dramatic fracture. It was a slow unraveling. A series of moments where I couldn't pretend anymore.

I had to choose between keeping peace on the surface and finding peace within myself.

With every hard truth I faced, I became lighter. Not because healing is easy, but because faking is heavier.

The Choice to Break the Pattern

Silence may start as protection, but eventually, it becomes a prison. It keeps you from being hurt, yes, but also from being known. Maybe most painfully, it keeps you from knowing yourself.

Breaking that silence isn't a single decision. It's the work of a lifetime. It means telling the truth even when your voice shakes. Choosing presence over avoidance. Letting go of performance in favor of connection.

Healing isn't about being perfect. It's about being real. It might just be the bravest thing you'll ever do—for yourself, for your children, for the women who came before you—is to say: *the silence stops here. This ends with me.*

Silence is a survival strategy. To break this chain, to stop the silence from passing to another generation, is the work of a lifetime. It means choosing to speak when your throat feels tight, choosing to be seen when everything in you wants to disappear, and choosing to say the hard thing even when it feels like it might shatter you.

Because in the end, the only way to break the inheritance of silence is to find your voice, no matter how long it's been buried.

Shadow Sheets

Personal Reflection:

1. Silent Agreements: What unspoken rules or quiet expectations shaped your early years? Were there things you felt you weren't allowed to express, even without being directly told?

   ----

2. Adapting vs. Authenticity: Think about the ways you've adapted to fit into your family, relationships, or social circles. What parts of yourself have you set aside or silenced to avoid conflict or disappointment?

   ----

3. Emotional Inheritance: What emotional habits or patterns do you think you may have absorbed from your family? How do these show up in the way you express (or hold back) your true feelings?

   ----

4. Performing for Others: Have you ever felt like you were acting a certain way to make others comfortable, even when it didn't feel true to who you are? What has this habit cost you over the years?

Generational Awareness:

5. Inherited Silence: Are there unspoken stories, family secrets, or emotional patterns that have shaped your understanding of yourself? How do these silences still echo in your life today?

----

6. Breaking the Cycle: If you have children (or plan to), what emotional patterns do you hope to break in your family? How can you start creating a more open, emotionally free environment for the next generation?

Reconnecting to Your Authentic Self:

7. Reclaiming Your Voice: Can you remember a time when you spoke your truth, even when it felt risky or uncomfortable? What did you learn about yourself in that moment?

   ----

8. Listening to Your Own Voice: Are there parts of yourself you've been silencing for too long? What would it feel like to let those parts speak again, even if just in a small way?

   ----

9. Finding the Real You: Who were you before you learned to filter, edit, or shrink yourself for others? What small steps could you take to reconnect with that version of yourself?

Setting Intentions for Healing:

10. Small, Brave Steps: What small, courageous action can you take this week to break a pattern of self-betrayal or silence? How can you honor your true voice, even if it feels unfamiliar at first?

Chapter 3:

THE COST OF SURVIVAL

"Sometimes, thriving is the greatest act of rebellion."

Survival isn't just about making it through the hard moments. It teaches you to anticipate storms, to brace for impact, to instinctively read the emotional weather around you. But survival has a cost. It's the quiet, often unconscious choices we make to shield ourselves, the roles we slip into to feel safe, and the ways we learn to anticipate every shift in our surroundings. These strategies, while protective in the beginning, can become the very chains that hold us back as adults. They shape our sense of self, our relationships, and our ability to stand in our own truth.

In the first two chapters, we explored the early formation of the shadow—those parts of ourselves we learned to hide, suppress, or deny to fit in, avoid conflict, or simply survive. We saw how early experiences teach us what parts of ourselves are acceptable and what parts are too much, too loud, or too complicated. Over time, these survival strategies, once adaptive, can become the habits that keep us stuck, disconnected, and living smaller than we were meant to.

Understanding the cost of survival means looking at the way these early adaptations form the foundation for many of the emotional patterns and relational struggles we carry into adulthood. It means recognizing that these strategies, while once protective, no longer serve the people we are becoming.

Patterns of Survival

Survival patterns rarely make themselves known. They slip into our lives quietly, almost unnoticed, much like the way a child learns to say "please" and "thank you," to wash their hands before dinner, or to stay silent when adults are speaking. These early reflexes become embedded in the way we navigate the world, shaping the tone we use, the way we present ourselves, and the way we filter our thoughts and actions without even realizing it. These aren't just habits; they become the quiet rhythms that guide us, the scripts we follow without question or doubt.

At first, these patterns don't seem like choices. They live below the surface, operating on a deeper level than conscious thought. They become automatic responses, shaping the way we interact with others long before we fully understand what we're trying to protect ourselves from. As time passes, these subtle acts of self-preservation start to blend into our sense of self, making it hard to distinguish between who we are and who we became in order to survive. These survival patterns, built on years of learned behavior, end up shaping us in ways we might not even recognize until we take the time to pause and reflect.

For some, this means learning to stay small, to fade into the background when the emotional temperature in a room rises. It means carefully modulating tone and volume, instinctively lowering your voice around someone prone to anger or choosing your words with precision to avoid conflict.

These aren't just behaviors—they become instinctive responses, shaping the way you move through the world.

Others learn to disappear in different ways, becoming experts at reading the emotional weather, anticipating shifts in mood, and adjusting accordingly. This heightened awareness becomes a form of emotional camouflage, a way to avoid standing out, to blend into the emotional landscape around you.

For others still, survival takes the form of perfectionism or overachievement, a relentless drive to control every detail, to excel in every environment, not because of a pure desire for success, but as a shield against the chaos or unpredictability they grew up around. In these cases, the pursuit of excellence becomes a form of emotional insulation, a way to create a sense of order in a world that once felt out of control.

For me, staying busy became second nature. My mother always encouraged me to stay active, signing me up for ballet, jazz, tap, gymnastics, band, and soccer. Cheerleading was the one thing I chose for myself, but even then, it became part of a pattern I couldn't fully see at the time. After my mom left, I clung to these activities—band, soccer, cheerleading. I didn't recognize it then, but these weren't just hobbies. They were distractions, ways to push through a loneliness I didn't yet know how to name. It wasn't just about filling my time. It was a way to avoid the silence, to escape the weight of unprocessed emotions I didn't yet have the tools to understand. Without realizing it, I was using constant motion as a shield, a way to stay out of reach of my own thoughts. These patterns weren't always things I chose for myself, but as a child, the environment you grow up in sets the tone for what feels normal.

Dating older guys in high school felt like an escape from the roles I felt trapped in, a chance to step outside the narrow definitions of who I was allowed to be. This wasn't about consciously rebelling or pushing boundaries, but about finding a version of myself that felt less restricted, even if just for a while. It offered a way to feel seen and valued, to step into a different version of myself—one that felt free, unburdened by the weight of expectations I didn't fully understand at the time.

Drinking, too, started as something that felt like freedom—a way to shake off the weight of self-consciousness, to slip into a version of myself that felt more like me without all the worries and anxiety. It became a way to blur the sharp edges of reality, to slip into the soft haze of connection and confidence, even if just for a night. I didn't recognize it then, but those choices weren't just youthful mistakes. They were early forms of unconscious attempts to avoid the discomfort of being fully present with myself. They didn't feel like problems then, just pieces of a life I was trying to shape into something more bearable, more fun, more socially connected.

Looking back, I can see how these patterns were survival strategies, not fixed parts of my identity. They were learned responses, shaped by the environment I grew up in, not fundamental truths about who I am. They helped me cope when I didn't have the tools to face my own pain, but they don't have to define who I become as an adult.

The challenge, of course, is that these survival patterns can feel so deeply woven into our sense of self that we hardly recognize them as choices. They become the background music of our lives, so familiar that we forget they ever had a starting point. But recognizing them for what they are is the first step in untangling them, in pulling apart the threads of habit and fear that keep us from fully inhabiting our lives.

Emotional Insulation and Early Coping

Emotional insulation often starts quietly, almost without notice. It's a way of protecting ourselves when we feel like our emotions might be too much, or when we've learned that showing vulnerability doesn't lead to understanding. It can happen in environments where expressing our feelings feels risky, or when our needs are dismissed over and over. At first, it might seem like a necessary defense, a way to keep ourselves from getting hurt. But over time, this pattern becomes a part of who we are, affecting how we relate to ourselves and the people around us. What once helped us survive can end up shaping our connections in ways we never intended.

For some, emotional insulation shows up as constant busyness a life packed with tasks and distractions that leave no space for self-reflection. Staying busy becomes a way to drown out the uncomfortable thoughts, to avoid the quiet that might bring up unresolved emotions. This can look like overcommitting to work or responsibilities, filling every moment with something to do in order to avoid the stillness that might force us to face the pain we've been avoiding.

For others, it might take the form of emotional detachment, keeping people at a safe distance, never fully allowing ourselves to be vulnerable. It can look like having a lot of acquaintances but no deep connections, or moving from one relationship to another without ever letting anyone get too close. The fear of being hurt keeps us from truly investing in others, keeping everyone at arm's length as a way to stay safe.

Some of us learn to emotionally insulate by becoming fiercely independent, refusing to rely on anyone else. On the surface, it may seem like strength, but beneath it lies the fear of being disappointed, abandoned, or exposed. This self-reliance acts as a barrier, a shield against the possibility of emotional hurt.

There are quieter ways to emotionally insulate, too—like using food, social media, or excessive exercise to numb ourselves. These habits may not seem as harmful as substance abuse or unhealthy relationships, but they can still serve the same purpose: keeping difficult emotions at a safe distance.

Even something as simple as emotionally disconnecting during a stressful moment can be a form of insulation. It's a way to create space between ourselves and the intensity of our feelings when they feel too much to handle. Over time, these patterns become automatic, influencing not just how we cope but how we show up in our lives, relationships, and work.

Recognizing these patterns means taking a close look at the ways we avoid discomfort, the ways we protect ourselves from the emotions we don't want to face. It's about seeing how we disconnect from others, and sometimes even from our own inner world. Becoming aware of these behaviors is the first step in breaking free from them, moving past the walls we built in childhood, and learning to live with more openness, authenticity, and connection as adults.

The Price of Survival

Every survival strategy comes at a cost. What begins as a way to shield ourselves from emotional pain can quietly become a barrier to truly living. These patterns, often developed out of necessity in childhood, follow us into adulthood, shaping how we move through the world. The same habits that once kept us safe can eventually become the chains that hold us back, keeping us small, disconnected, and living smaller lives than we were meant to.

This cost could show up as emotional insulation—the constant busyness, the endless distractions, the carefully curated chaos that keeps them from sitting still with their own thoughts. It might look like overcommitting to work, filling every spare moment with tasks, or endlessly scrolling through social media to avoid the discomfort of stillness. These habits can feel productive, even necessary, but they slowly erode the ability to connect, to be fully present, and to know oneself.

Clinging to control becomes a way to feel safe in a world that once felt unpredictable or chaotic. For some, it takes the shape of perfectionism—a constant drive for flawlessness, as if achieving the perfect outcome will protect them from feelings of inadequacy or the fear of being judged. For others, it might show up as obsessive organization, meticulous planning, or the need to manage every detail, all in an effort to shield themselves from the chaos they once felt powerless against.

At first, this desire for control can create a sense of order, a feeling of being on top of things. But over time, it often leads to burnout, strained relationships, and a constant hum of anxiety. What begins as a strategy for feeling secure turns into a heavy burden, as it's a trade-off: freedom for the illusion of safety? And in the end, it's a bargain that leaves them feeling trapped by their own high standards, constantly striving for an ideal that never seems to arrive.

Becoming masters of people-pleasing, learning early on to anticipate the needs of others, to read the emotional weather in a room, and to mold themselves into whatever version of themselves will keep the peace. They become experts at self-editing, constantly putting others first, often at the cost of their own needs and desires. This constant self-sacrifice can lead to resentment, burnout, and a deep sense of being unseen, even in close relationships. It's the slow, quiet loss of self that happens when too much time is spent performing for others and not enough time being true to oneself.

Some swing in the opposite direction, choosing hyper-independence as a form of self-protection. They refuse to rely on anyone, pushing people away before they have the chance to get too close, or avoiding emotional intimacy to protect themselves from the risk of being hurt. This fierce self-reliance can look like strength, but it often leads to isolation, loneliness, and a slow erosion of meaningful connection. It's a way of saying, "I don't need anyone," when what they really mean is, "I can't bear the thought of being let down."

Turning to numbing behaviors—whether its alcohol, drugs, food, gambling, or even excessive exercise—often begins as a way to soften the sharp edges of life. These habits offer a temporary escape, dulling the ache of emotions we haven't processed or giving us a false sense of control in an unpredictable world. But numbing can also take subtler forms, like emotionally shutting down, avoiding tough conversations, or immersing ourselves in work or hobbies to sidestep the discomfort of facing who we really are.

The problem with numbing, however, is that it comes at a heavy price. It doesn't just disconnect us from the pain we're trying to avoid, it distances us from the things that bring us joy, our passions, and even our sense of purpose. It leaves us living on the outskirts of our own lives, never fully experiencing or engaging with what truly matters. We lose the ability to feel deeply, not just the pain, but also the beauty and richness of life.

Ultimately, the greatest cost of these survival strategies is the slow, quiet erosion of the self. It's the gradual loss of one's own voice beneath the noise of distraction, the dulling of one's own desires beneath the weight of constant performance, and the slow fading of one's own truth beneath the layers of armor worn to feel safe.

The truth is, these survival strategies might feel like second nature, but they aren't unchangeable parts of who we are. They are coping mechanisms, responses to an earlier life we may no longer be living, and they come with a price. They steal our ability to be fully present, to connect deeply, and to live without constant self-editing. They keep us from our own truth, leaving us trapped in roles we didn't consciously choose.

But the fact that these patterns are learned means they can also be unlearned. Recognizing them is the first, essential step. It's the moment you stop mistaking survival strategies for personality, the moment you see that the habits that once protected you have become the very walls keeping you small.

Breaking free from these patterns means more than just letting go of the behaviors that no longer serve you. It means finding your way back to yourself. It means learning to sit with discomfort instead of drowning it out. It means choosing connection over isolation, presence over distraction, and authenticity over performance. This isn't a one-time decision. It's a practice, a commitment to yourself that you make every day. It's the slow, steady work of reclaiming your voice, your power, and your sense of self.

Breaking the Cycle

Breaking the cycle isn't just about letting go of the behaviors that no longer serve you. It's about reclaiming the parts of yourself that got buried under years of survival. For so long, you've lived behind layers of protection, hiding behind roles and masks, but true freedom is about peeling those layers away and allowing your real self to breathe again. It's about finding the courage to stop performing, to risk being seen, and to trust that you don't need to hide to be safe.

This journey begins with recognizing that survival served its purpose—it helped you make it through. But it doesn't have to define you forever. You don't have to stay trapped in patterns that no longer serve you, locked in roles you outgrew long ago. The power to change, to step out of the shadows of your past, and to stop pretending for others is already within you. You can choose to live for yourself now.

Breaking the cycle is about listening to the quiet voice inside that's been silenced for too long. It's about giving yourself permission to be who you truly are, without second-guessing your worth or fearing rejection. It's about taking up space unapologetically, standing firm in your truth, even if it feels foreign at first. It's about feeling your emotions deeply, instead of numbing them; speaking your truth, instead of swallowing it down; and setting clear boundaries, instead of endlessly compromising.

The real work is in trusting that you are worthy of peace, joy, and love, just as you are. It's about choosing to live authentically, even when it feels uncomfortable, because in doing so, you begin to uncover the parts of yourself that have been hidden for too long. Breaking the cycle is the courageous act of letting yourself be fully alive again.

But what does that actually look like in practice?

1. Building Awareness

Breaking a cycle starts with awareness. You can't change what you can't see. This means paying attention to the ways you shrink, hide, or edit yourself to feel safe. Notice the moments when you hold back, when you say yes out of obligation, or when you stay quiet to keep the peace. Catch yourself in the act of people-pleasing, perfectionism, or emotional detachment, and recognize these behaviors for what they are—survival strategies, not personality traits.

2. Challenging Old Beliefs

Next, challenge the beliefs that keep these patterns in place. What have you come to believe about yourself in order to survive? That you have to be perfect to be loved? That your needs are a burden? That vulnerability is weakness? These beliefs might have felt true once, but they are not unchangeable truths. They are old scripts, echoes of a past you don't have to keep living in.

3. Setting Boundaries and Reclaiming Your Voice

Breaking the cycle also means reclaiming your right to say no, to take up space, and to prioritize your own needs. This is about setting boundaries without guilt, speaking your truth without apology, and letting yourself be seen without constantly editing your words or actions to make others more comfortable. This might feel awkward or even terrifying at first, but it's a critical part of breaking free from old roles.

4. Choosing Connection Over Protection

It also means learning to lean into connection, even when it feels vulnerable. This might mean letting people see the messy, unpolished parts of you. It means being willing to risk closeness, to trust that not everyone will hurt you, and to believe that you are worthy of deep, meaningful relationships.

5. Making Peace with Discomfort

Breaking a cycle isn't comfortable. It means sitting with the discomfort you once ran from, letting yourself feel the full weight of your emotions without numbing, distracting, or disconnecting. It means learning to sit in the stillness you once avoided, to hear your own thoughts without judgment, and to let yourself be fully present in your own life.

6. Practicing Self-Compassion

Finally, it means being kind to yourself in the process. Breaking these patterns is not a straight path, and there will be days when you fall back into old habits, when you choose distraction over presence or silence over truth. That's okay. Growth is messy, imperfect, and deeply human. Give yourself the grace to stumble as you learn to walk in a new way.

This is not a one-time decision. It's a practice, a commitment to yourself that you make every day. It's the slow, steady work of reclaiming your voice, your power, and your sense of self. It means letting go of the need to be perfect, to always be strong, or to constantly prove your worth. It means choosing to live, not just survive.

The reward for this work is a life that feels fully yours—a life where you are no longer just reacting to the past, but actively creating a future that feels true to who you are.

Finding Your Way Home

The next chapter is about going deeper—digging into the roots of your survival strategies, tracing them back to the first bonds that shaped your sense of self. It's about unearthing the early stories you absorbed about love, safety, and belonging, and seeing how those foundational lessons shaped the patterns you still carry today.

This is a journey of coming home to yourself. It's about shedding the masks you wore to survive, stepping out of the roles you were taught to play, and choosing to stand fully in your truth. It's about reclaiming the parts of yourself that got buried beneath the weight of survival, and learning to trust that you don't have to hide to be safe.

It means asking the bigger questions:

- Who taught you what love feels like?
- What messages did you absorb about your worth, your needs, and your place in the world?
- Where did you first learn to shrink, to silence yourself, to hide parts of who you are?

This is where you get to rewrite those stories. To challenge the early narratives that told you to stay small, to blend in, and to silence parts of yourself just to feel safe. It's about finding the courage to stand fully in your truth, even when it feels unfamiliar or risky.

This work is about more than just breaking old habits.

It's about reclaiming your life, your voice, and your power.

It's about finding the person you were before the world taught you to doubt yourself, to question your worth, to hide your true self.

It's about finding your way back to yourself, the version of you that existed before survival became your default. Because you deserve more than just survival. You deserve to thrive.

Shadow Sheets

Personal Reflection:

1. Coping Habits: When you feel overwhelmed, stressed, or emotionally uncomfortable, what do you tend to do to feel better, even if just for a moment?

   ----

2. Distracting Yourself: Are there habits, routines, or behaviors you rely on to avoid uncomfortable thoughts or emotions? These might include staying busy, overworking, constantly socializing, or retreating into a hobby.

   ----

3. Creating Emotional Distance: Are there times when you hold back from sharing your true feelings or distance yourself from others to protect yourself? What do you do when you feel emotionally exposed or vulnerable?

   ----

4. Hidden Patterns: Can you think of choices you've made or habits you've developed that, looking back, might have been ways to avoid pain, protect yourself, or keep others at a distance?

Patterns and Their Impact:

5. Long-Term Effects: How have these coping strategies shaped the way you handle relationships, stress, or conflict? Do they help you feel more secure, or do they sometimes make you feel more disconnected?

   ----

6. Early Training: Are there ways of thinking or behaving that you once thought were just "who you are," but now recognize as learned responses to past experiences?

Breaking the Cycle:

7. Recognizing the Cost: When you think about the ways you've coped, what has it cost you? In your relationships? In your sense of self? In your ability to feel truly connected to others?

----

8. Trying New Approaches: What are some healthier ways of coping you could try that don't involve avoiding, distracting, or distancing yourself?

Moving Forward:

9. Finding the Real You: If you stopped distracting yourself, avoiding certain feelings, or hiding parts of yourself, who might you rediscover?

----

10. Exploring New Ways of Being: What would it feel like to approach life with a little less armor, a little more curiosity, and a bit more trust in yourself?

Chapter 4:

THE MOTHER ARCHETYPE

When we talk about the journey of self-discovery and shadow work, it's impossible to ignore the profound influence of the mother archetype. This is where our sense of self begins to form, where we first learn who we are in relation to others and what it means to belong. It's the first emotional blueprint we inherit, shaping our understanding of love, safety, and connection long before we have words to describe them. This chapter is about exploring that foundational relationship, not just with our biological mothers, but with the internalized mother figure that lives within us all.

The mother archetype is more than just a reflection of our childhood caregivers. It's a psychological pattern that shapes our emotional landscape, teaching us our earliest lessons about trust, worth, and belonging. It's the origin of our first attachments, the template for how we learn to receive love and comfort, and the framework for our deepest fears of rejection, abandonment, and unworthiness.

But like all powerful archetypes, the mother has two sides. She is both the nurturer and the devourer, the giver of life and the one who can withhold it. She can be the source of deep, unconditional love, but also the root of our earliest wounds. Understanding this duality is essential for anyone seeking to break free from the unconscious patterns that keep us trapped in cycles of self-doubt, emotional repression, and addictive behaviors.

As we move through this chapter, we'll explore the complex ways the mother archetype shapes our inner worlds, how it influences our relationships, and how it sets the stage for the shadows we carry into adulthood. We'll look at the ways early attachment wounds can manifest as addictive behaviors, emotional numbing, or self-sabotage, and how recognizing these patterns can be the first step toward healing and reclaiming our sense of self.

This work isn't just about understanding the past. It's about recognizing the echoes of those early attachments in the present — the ways they continue to shape our choices, our relationships, and our sense of self-worth. It's about breaking the cycles that keep us stuck, reclaiming the parts of ourselves we have been taught to deny, and learning to stand fully in our truth, even when it feels unfamiliar or risky.

To do this, we'll first explore the psychological foundations of the mother archetype, drawing on both Jungian theory and modern attachment science. We'll examine the emotional imprints left by our earliest attachments, the scripts we carry into adulthood, and the shadows that form when our early needs go unmet. This chapter will also begin to bridge the gap between survival strategies and deeper attachment wounds, setting the stage for the exploration of addictive behaviors, repression, and emotional wounds that will come in later chapters.

If we are to truly understand our shadows and reclaim the parts of ourselves we have been taught to deny, we must start here, in the place where our first emotional imprints were made, in the relationship that set the tone for all others.

Introduction to the Mother Archetype

The mother archetype is deeply woven into both mythology and psychology. It stands as one of the most enduring and complex symbols we encounter in human storytelling and our journey toward understanding ourselves. The idea was popularized by Swiss psychiatrist Carl Gustav Jung, who first introduced archetypes as universal, inherited patterns of thought and behavior. These patterns arise from what Jung described as the collective unconscious, a shared psychic inheritance that transcends both time and culture.

Jung believed these archetypes serve as the building blocks of the human psyche. They shape how we perceive and experience the world on the most fundamental level. Each archetype has its own unique influence over the way we move through life, guiding us in ways we often don't even realize.

Of these archetypes, the mother stands out as one of the most essential. She embodies creation, nourishment, protection, and unconditional love. The mother is the first archetype we encounter in our lives, and her presence stretches far beyond the biological relationship with our mothers. She represents the internalized sense of care and safety, the feeling of belonging that molds our deepest beliefs about our worth and emotional security.

Across the world, the mother archetype appears in countless forms. We can see her in the nurturing figures like the Virgin Mary, Demeter, and Gaia, each one representing a different aspect of life-giving love. But we also encounter the fiercer sides of this archetype, found in the protective deities like Kali and Sekhmet, whose power is as formidable as it is transformative. These mythic figures illustrate the full spectrum of the mother archetype, showing us that motherhood isn't just about gentleness and care, it's also about transformation, sometimes even destruction, in order to create anew.

Jung's early exploration of the mother archetype revealed its profound impact on our psychology. He emphasized that this archetype represents more than just the physical mother. It also embodies the internalized, often unconscious image of care and containment that forms within each of us. This internalized mother serves as a foundational template for our earliest emotional experiences, shaping how we view ourselves, our expectations in relationships, and our ability to connect with others on a deep, authentic level. It is the source from which our first feelings of safety, love, and connection flow. However, it can also be the root of deep emotional wounds when those basic needs are left unmet.

Over the years, modern therapists have built upon Jung's original insights, adding more layers of understanding through attachment theory, developmental psychology, and trauma research. Today, the mother archetype is seen as a living, evolving framework rather than a static symbol. It reflects the complexities of early relational experiences. It can represent the nurturing, life-giving aspects of care, but it can also reveal the darker, more challenging dynamics such as control, overprotection, neglect, or emotional enmeshment. These early relational patterns have a lasting influence, often showing up in our adult relationships. They shape the choices we make, the fears we carry, and the emotional patterns we continue to repeat.

Therapists and self-development practitioners today recognize that our relationship with the internalized mother plays a significant role in many aspects of our lives. It influences everything from our self-esteem and emotional resilience to our ability to experience intimacy and express ourselves authentically. For those who grew up with inconsistent, rejecting, or emotionally harmful experiences with their mothers, the wounds from this early bond can linger and affect their adult lives in profound ways. These unresolved feelings often cast long shadows, shaping how we relate to ourselves and others.

In cases like these, the journey of reclaiming one's true self often means confronting and reimagining the internalized mother figure. It involves breaking free from the unconscious scripts and patterns that no longer serve us. The healing process becomes about rewriting the emotional narratives we've carried for so long, creating healthier, more fulfilling relationships with ourselves and those around us.

Seeing the mother archetype through this broader, more integrated lens offers a powerful tool for self-discovery, healing, and personal growth. It encourages us to view our earliest relational patterns not as permanent limitations, but as the raw material for meaningful change. As we explore this chapter, we'll dive into how these early imprints form, how they continue to influence our adult lives, and how we can begin the work of untangling the unconscious patterns that leave us stuck, disconnected, or afraid to fully embrace life.

The Psychological Blueprint of Motherhood

Our earliest attachments form the psychological blueprint for how we move through the world. These first bonds don't just teach us how to connect with others — they also teach us how to connect with ourselves. They shape the voice we carry in our minds, the internal mother who whispers to us long after we've left our childhood homes. This internal mother becomes the filter through which we interpret the world, the voice that tells us whether we are safe, worthy, or enough.

For some, this internal mother is a gentle guide, offering words of comfort and reassurance in moments of doubt. For others, she is a harsher critic, echoing the fears and judgments of early caregivers, repeating the unspoken messages of conditional love and unspoken expectations.

When we are young, we absorb these messages without question. They become the background noise of our minds, the silent agreements that shape our sense of self-worth and emotional safety. If we were nurtured and valued, our internal voice might reflect that same sense of security and belonging. But if we grew up in chaos, in emotional storms where our needs were overlooked or punished, that voice can become a harsh judge, a relentless reminder of our perceived inadequacies.

I can still hear the echoes of the voices that shaped my early understanding of worth. I remember the sting of harsh words, the way my attempts to express my own needs or fears were often met with dismissal or criticism. I learned to anticipate disapproval, to shrink my needs, to soften my voice, to become small enough to avoid triggering someone else's anger. Over time, this became my default, a survival strategy that felt like self-protection but slowly eroded my sense of self.

These early messages don't just shape our inner world. They become the scripts we carry into adulthood, influencing our relationships, our self-image, and our ability to set healthy boundaries. They become the reflexes that guide our decisions, the quiet voices that tell us when to speak up or stay silent, when to risk connection or retreat into isolation.

It's not just the obvious, harsh criticisms that leave a mark. Sometimes, it's the unspoken lessons — the quiet disapproval, the withheld affection, the subtle signals that our emotions are too much or our needs are a burden. These are the emotional blueprints that set the stage for our shadows, the unconscious patterns that can follow us into every relationship, every job, and every moment of self-doubt.

The internal mother isn't just a reflection of our childhood caregivers. She is a psychological construct, a deeply ingrained set of beliefs about our worth, our safety, and our place in the world. She is the voice we have internalized, the one we hear when we are afraid, when we doubt ourselves, or when we struggle to feel deserving of love.

These early attachments, these first emotional imprints, become the foundation for the survival strategies we later adopt. They shape the way we learn to soothe ourselves, the way we cope with stress, and the ways we seek or avoid connection. They become the roots of our shadows, the hidden scripts that guide our lives until we become aware of them and choose to rewrite them.

The Dual Nature of the Mother Archetype

The mother archetype, like all powerful symbols, carries both light and shadow. She is the source of life, the giver of comfort, and the first face we come to trust. But, she can also be the source of our earliest fears—the first figure to introduce us to rejection, disappointment, and emotional withdrawal. This dual nature lies at the heart of the mother archetype, shaping not only our earliest attachments but also our lifelong understanding of safety, love, and belonging.

Psychologically, we can understand this complexity through the idea of the "good mother" and the "bad mother." These are not literal judgments, but rather internalized experiences that form the foundation of our emotional lives. The good mother represents the nurturing and supportive presence that makes us feel safe, valued, and seen. She is the one who comforts our tears, celebrates our first steps, and holds space for our growing independence. This is the mother who teaches us that we are enough just as we are, that our needs are valid, and that our very presence is a gift.

The shadow side of the mother archetype can be just as powerful, even if it's more difficult to see. This side is the one that withholds love, punishes vulnerability, or demands emotional loyalty in ways that can feel suffocating. It's the voice inside our heads that tells us we must earn love, that we have to prove our worth every single day. It's the quiet fear that being ourselves might come at the cost of being loved. This is the mother who, whether she meant to or not, teaches us to hide parts of ourselves—to shrink back, to stay silent, and to mold ourselves into whatever shape will keep the peace, even if it means losing ourselves in the process.

For some, this dynamic plays out in subtle, almost imperceptible moments. A look of quiet disapproval after a poor grade, the tightening of a jaw when emotions get too big, or a hug that feels less like comfort and more like a trap. These moments leave an imprint, a feeling that we are loved only when we're "good," only when we behave in a way that meets expectations. For others, the shadow side is much more overt—love is withheld as a form of discipline, emotional support becomes conditional, and vulnerability is something to fear. It becomes clear: to be open, to show weakness, is to risk losing the love we so desperately need.

These early experiences leave marks on us that run deep, shaping the scripts we unknowingly carry into adulthood. They become the quiet backdrop of our relationships, the unspoken rules that guide how we seek connection, express our needs, and protect our hearts. We learn to read between the lines, to anticipate emotional storms, and to brace ourselves for the possibility of rejection.

Psychologists have long understood this duality, recognizing that our first encounters with care and conflict shape the blueprints we follow in our adult relationships. It's why we sometimes choose partners who mirror the wounds of our childhood or find ourselves falling into patterns of self-sacrifice or emotional withdrawal, even when we don't fully understand why. These patterns are etched in us, invisible yet powerful.

In this way, the mother archetype serves as both a guide and a ghost. She shapes our sense of self, our capacity for intimacy, and our ability to stand in our own truth. She is the soft whisper that reassures us: "You are loved, you are enough." But she's also the shadow that warns: "Don't ask for too much, don't be too much, or you'll end up alone."

Understanding this duality is crucial for anyone hoping to break free from the unconscious patterns that keep us stuck in cycles of self-doubt, emotional repression, and unhealthy behaviors. It's about seeing the whole picture—the comfort and the chaos, the nurture and the neglect, the love and the fear. Only by acknowledging both sides can we begin to untangle the threads of our early attachments and reclaim the parts of ourselves we've been taught to deny.

Personal Reflections on the Mother Wound and Internalizing the Mother Voice

The mother's voice doesn't merely echo in our minds—it infiltrates the very fabric of how we perceive ourselves and the world around us. It's not just the words she spoke, but the weight in her tone, the timing, the rhythm of each unspoken expectation. I know for me, the pressure wasn't subtle. It came in clear, unambiguous messages: be good, be helpful, always perform, and always meet expectations without protest. It taught me that love and approval weren't unconditional, but something to be earned. My worth wasn't a given; it had to be proven—time and time again.

But for others, this internalized voice might manifest differently. For some, it's the ceaseless drive to excel, to constantly achieve, to be seen as worthy through accomplishments. For others, it's the pressure to avoid conflict, to keep things smooth, to always place the needs of others above their own. It can show up as the gnawing fear of being a burden, an unspoken expectation to remain composed, to suppress desires, and to believe that your needs, your desires, your feelings are always secondary to the comfort and peace of those around you. It's the silent belief that your presence is only acceptable if it causes no disruption, no disturbance.

This voice can also take the form of a deeply ingrained sense of responsibility, one that compels you to control the emotional atmosphere around you, to fix, to soothe, to make everything right—even at the cost of your own well-being. It's the silent script that guides how you respond to stress, navigate relationships, and measure your own worth. It's why you might find yourself apologizing for things that aren't your fault, questioning your value before speaking up, or doubting your right to take up space in a room.

For some, this inner voice isn't just critical or demanding. It can also be protective—an intense, almost fierce directive that urges you to stay sharp, stay prepared, to always be alert to potential threats. It's that part of you that learned early on to take responsibility for the comfort of others, to absorb their discomfort without a second thought, and to anticipate problems before they ever emerge.

And the truth is, the echoes of these early lessons don't simply fade with time. They shape how we move through the world, the expectations we hold for ourselves, and the way we talk to ourselves in moments of doubt. They become the internal scripts that dictate how we relate to our own worth, our decisions, and ultimately, our sense of self. These voices don't just whisper—they carve out a path for us, one that influences every choice, every relationship, and every step we take.

For some, this internalized voice becomes a relentless drive to be good, to be needed, to earn approval—no matter the cost. It shows up as over-functioning in relationships, constantly giving without asking for anything in return, or placing others' needs ahead of your own in an attempt to feel worthy. For others, it manifests as a quiet but powerful fear of intimacy—an instinct to pull away when someone gets too close, a reflex to withdraw when vulnerability feels like a dangerous risk.

These early imprints don't just fade with time. They become woven into the very architecture of your mind, shaping how you move through the world, how you speak to yourself, and the standards you hold yourself to. They dictate how you form connections, navigate conflict, and ultimately, how you measure your own worth. These patterns may feel like second nature, ingrained in your very being, but in truth, they are the echoes of early emotional fractures—subtle wounds that laid the groundwork for struggles with attachment, self-repression, and self-doubt. They are the silent scripts that govern how we relate to others and, perhaps more poignantly, how we relate to ourselves.

Healing the Mother Wound and Reparenting Yourself

Healing the mother wound is not just about processing old pain or letting go of the past. It's about learning to mother yourself, to provide the comfort, protection, and unconditional support that may have been missing in your early years. It's about becoming the nurturing presence you needed when you were young, and reclaiming the parts of yourself that you had to bury to survive.

Reparenting isn't about blaming your mother or rewriting history. It's about recognizing the gaps, the unmet needs, and the emotional wounds that shaped you, and choosing to fill those spaces with a more compassionate, supportive voice. It's about giving yourself the love, acceptance, and validation that you may have searched for in others but never fully received. This process is essential for breaking the cycles of emotional repression, self-doubt, and self-sabotage that often stem from these early wounds.

Learning to mother yourself means setting boundaries, reclaiming your voice, and finding your own sense of worth outside the roles and expectations you may have internalized. It means choosing to trust your own instincts, to prioritize your own needs, and to break the habit of putting others' comfort ahead of your own well-being.

For me, this journey began when I realized that my self-worth had been tangled up in the expectations of others, that my sense of value was too often measured by how well I could keep the peace, anticipate others' needs, and avoid being a burden. It meant learning to say no without guilt, to set boundaries without fear, and to let myself feel the full range of my emotions without trying to edit them to make others more comfortable.

For others, this process might look different. It might mean learning to speak up for yourself, to stop apologizing for taking up space, or to release the need to earn love through over-giving or self-sacrifice. It might mean finding the courage to walk away from relationships that no longer serve you, to stop performing for approval, and to start living for yourself.

Reparenting isn't a one-time decision. It's a daily practice, a commitment to yourself that you make again and again, even when it feels uncomfortable or unfamiliar. It's about choosing to hear the whispers of your own mind, to trust the voice you've silenced, and to reclaim the parts of you that were left behind.

Moving Forward

Understanding the mother archetype goes beyond simply reflecting on our childhoods or analyzing our relationship with our biological mothers. It's about recognizing the deep, often unconscious imprints that shape how we navigate the world, how we connect with others, and how we see ourselves. It's about bringing awareness to the patterns we may have inherited—emotional reflexes we developed as a way to survive—and the power we have to rewrite these scripts as adults.

Self-awareness is the first step. It's the moment you break free from autopilot, the point at which you choose to challenge the internalized voices that have shaped your sense of self. It's about noticing when you shrink in the face of conflict, when you silence your own needs to keep the peace, or when you fall into patterns of seeking love and approval at the expense of your own well-being. It's about being brutally honest with yourself—about the roles you play, the masks you wear, and the truths you bury in order to feel safe. Only then can you begin to heal and create new narratives, ones that empower you to live authentically and reclaim your sense of worth.

Emotional honesty is the second step. It's about learning to sit with your feelings without judgment, to name the parts of yourself you have been taught to deny, and to speak the truths you have swallowed for too long. It's about finding the courage to feel, even when it's uncomfortable, and to confront the shadows that have kept you small.

Self-compassion is the final step. It's the practice of treating yourself with the same kindness, patience, and understanding that you might offer to a friend. It's about learning to mother yourself in the ways you may not have been mothered, to nurture the parts of you that feel unworthy, and to offer yourself the comfort you may have spent a lifetime seeking from others.

As we move into the next chapter, we will begin to explore the deeper roots of our emotional patterns, tracing them back to the earliest attachments and the foundational relationships that shaped our emotional landscapes. We will look at the powerful influence of early attachment wounds, the ways we learn to survive in environments where our needs aren't fully met, and the impact of those early imprints on our adult relationships.

This journey isn't just about surviving. It's about reclaiming your life, your voice, and your power. It's about breaking free from the roles you were taught to play and finding the courage to step into your full, authentic self. Because you deserve more than just survival. You deserve to thrive.

Shadow Sheet

Psychological Foundations of the Mother Archetype

1. How did your earliest experiences with your mother or primary caregiver shape your understanding of safety, love, and belonging? What messages about your worth did you absorb in those formative years?

   ----

2. In what ways have you internalized the emotional patterns, fears, or expectations you observed in your mother figure? How have these patterns influenced your self-image and relationships?

   ----

3. How has your relationship with your mother influenced the way you respond to stress, set boundaries, or navigate conflict?

Internalized Mother Voice

4. What unspoken rules or silent agreements did you learn from your mother about love, acceptance, and emotional safety? How do these early lessons show up in your current relationships?

----

5. Reflect on the tone of your inner dialogue. Does it echo the supportive, nurturing side of the mother archetype, or does it carry a more critical, demanding tone? How has this internal voice shaped your self-worth?

----

6. If you could rewrite the internalized voice of your mother, what would you want it to say to you now? What affirmations or messages would you choose to replace the old scripts?

Early Emotional Imprints and Attachment Wounds

7. What parts of yourself did you learn to hide, silence, or minimize to avoid conflict, disapproval, or rejection in your early years? How has this shaped your adult identity?

----

8. In what ways have you felt the need to earn love, approval, or acceptance in your relationships? How might this be connected to your early experiences with

----

----

9. How has your relationship with your mother influenced your ability to feel secure, emotionally open, and authentic in your adult relationships?

Reclaiming Your Authentic Self

10. As you reflect on your journey of self-discovery, what would it mean for you to truly reclaim your sense of worth, separate from the roles and expectations you internalized as a child? What would it feel like to stand fully in your truth, even when it challenges the scripts you've been taught to follow?

Chapter 5:

WHEN LOVE FEELS DANGEROUS

"The body doesn't crave what's healthy. It craves what's familiar—even when it hurts"

The Cost of Unsafe Attachments

What happens when the people we needed most were also the ones we had to protect ourselves from? Not because they were monsters, but because their love came with conditions, inconsistencies, or silent undercurrents of pain. This is the heartbreak of unsafe attachment—the kind that teaches us early on that love can't be trusted, and neither can we.

In the last chapter, we explored the mother archetype and how our earliest emotional blueprints are formed. We looked at what it means to internalize the unmet needs, projections, and unconscious pain of our caregivers. Now, we turn toward what those early experiences actually cost us—how they shape our strategies for survival, our beliefs about love, and our ability to feel safe in connection.

For many of us, survival meant becoming who we needed to be—quiet, high-achieving, agreeable, or resistant. These weren't choices. They were quiet negotiations with our nervous system to avoid abandonment or feel less alone in chaos.

This chapter is about those negotiations. We'll explore the science of attachment and how early relational wounds lead to coping strategies that look like personality traits—but are actually trauma responses in disguise. We'll unpack the subtle ways love can become dangerous and how that danger rewires our sense of safety, not just in relationships, but in our own bodies.

You'll begin to see how your patterns—whether it's people-pleasing, hyper-independence, emotional withdrawal, or self-sabotage—aren't signs that something is wrong with you. They're evidence that something happened to you.

As we go deeper, you'll start to reclaim the part of you that learned how to survive... but is finally ready to learn how to feel safe.

The Science of Attachment and Early Survival Patterns

Attachment theory helps us understand something we've all felt but rarely know how to explain: why we behave the way we do in relationships, especially when emotions run high.

At its core, attachment is about safety—specifically, whether we felt safe, soothed, and consistently cared for by our primary caregivers during early childhood. These first relationships shape the blueprint that our nervous system uses to determine if the world (and the people in it) are safe, predictable, and emotionally available.

Psychologists have identified four main attachment styles. These aren't labels or boxes. They're strategies we use to seek connection—or shield ourselves when it's missing. They begin forming as early as infancy and deeply influence how we relate to others throughout life.

1. Secure Attachment

How it develops: When a child experiences consistent, responsive care—when their emotional and physical needs are met without punishment, confusion, or chaos—their nervous system learns that connection is safe. The caregiver doesn't need to be perfect, just "good enough" most of the time.

How it feels: People with secure attachment tend to feel comfortable with closeness and independence. They trust others, regulate emotions well, and are usually resilient in the face of conflict or change.

Why it matters: Secure attachment creates a sense of inner safety. It teaches the child: "I can rely on others, and I am worthy of love."

2. Anxious Attachment (also called Preoccupied Attachment)

How it develops: When a caregiver is inconsistent—sometimes nurturing, sometimes distant or distracted—the child becomes hyper-attuned to the caregiver's emotional state. They may cry louder, cling harder, or become emotionally intense to try to secure attention.

How it feels: As adults, anxiously attached individuals often fear abandonment. They may feel "needy," overthink relationships, or need constant reassurance. Their emotions feel overwhelming and hard to regulate alone.

Why it matters: This child learns: "Love is unpredictable. I have to work hard to keep it." The nervous system becomes wired for anxiety and hypervigilance in relationships.

3. Avoidant Attachment (also called Dismissive Attachment)

How it develops: When a caregiver is emotionally unavailable, dismissive, or consistently discourages emotional expression, the child learns to suppress their needs. Expressing vulnerability might have been met with indifference, shame, or even punishment.

How it feels: As adults, avoidantly attached people often pride themselves on independence and self-sufficiency. They may struggle with emotional intimacy, avoid vulnerability, or feel uncomfortable when others depend on them.

Why it matters: This child learns: "My needs won't be met, so I'll stop having them." The nervous system shuts down emotional expression to avoid further pain or rejection.

4. Disorganized Attachment (also called Fearful-Avoidant Attachment)

How it develops: When a child's caregiver is both a source of comfort and fear—such as in situations of abuse, trauma, addiction, or chronic emotional unpredictability—the child has no consistent strategy. They are caught between the instinct to seek safety and the instinct to protect themselves from danger.

How it feels: As adults, people with disorganized attachment may experience intense inner conflict in relationships. They may crave closeness but also fear it. Their relationships may feel chaotic, with patterns of push-pull, mistrust, and emotional reactivity.

Why it matters: This child learns: "The person I need to feel safe is also the one who scares me." The nervous system becomes stuck in a loop of confusion, alternating between fight, flight, and freeze responses.

Attachment Styles Are Fluid, Not Fixed

It's easy to read about attachment styles and want to pick just one.

To find the box that feels most accurate, and finally understand: "Ah, this is why I am the way I am."

But the truth is—most people aren't just one style.

Attachment styles are adaptive survival strategies, not personality types. They're shaped by early relationships, but they're also constantly being updated by new experiences, new wounds, and new healing.

A person might:

- Feel secure in friendships, but anxious in romantic relationships
- Show up as avoidant in conflict, but fawning when emotionally triggered
- Move between chasing and withdrawing in the same relationship—especially when a deep wound is activated

These patterns often shift depending on:

- Who we're with
- How safe we feel
- How resourced we are
- What our nervous system has learned to expect

The goal isn't to identify with a single style forever.

The goal is to recognize how these patterns show up, so we can begin to unlearn them—and move toward internal safety, emotional regulation, and earned secure attachment.

Attachment Styles Overview

Attachment Style	Core Belief	Behavior in Relationships
Secure	I am worthy of love and connection.	Open, trusting, emotionally regulated
Anxious (Preoccupied)	I must cling to others to feel safe.	Clingy, worried, needs constant reassurance
Avoidant (Dismissive)	I can only rely on myself.	Distant, self-reliant, emotionally detached
Disorganized (Fearful)	I want closeness, but fear it will hurt me.	Push-pull patterns, emotional chaos, high anxiety

The Body Keeps the Score

These early attachment styles don't just shape our psychology—they shape our biology. The nervous system becomes programmed to respond to closeness, conflict, and emotional cues based on the safety (or lack of it) we experienced as children.

When our needs weren't consistently met, the body often internalized it as danger. Over time, we adapted. We became who we needed to be to survive emotionally. These were learned patterns designed to keep us connected—even at the cost of ourselves.

But what protected us in childhood can limit us in adulthood. The same attachment pattern that once kept us safe might now be the reason we fear intimacy, sabotage connection, or stay in emotionally unsafe relationships.

Personal Story Prompt:

Reflect on a moment in adulthood when you noticed yourself reacting strongly to a relationship trigger—maybe you shut down, chased after someone, avoided a conversation, or felt a wave of panic over something small. What early attachment pattern might that reaction be connected to?

Mine:

When My Old Wounds Get Loud

I knew something had shifted before I could explain it. The energy between us felt... off. He didn't say anything harsh, but suddenly, I felt far away from him—even sitting right beside him. Just like that, my chest got tight, my mind started racing, and the old fear kicked in.

Did I do something wrong? Should I reach out? Stay quiet? Am I being too sensitive again?

It's wild how fast I can go from calm to spiraling—trying to fix it, trying to reconnect, trying to hold on—while secretly feeling like I'm losing him.

When I don't get the reassurance I'm craving, I tend to shut down. I pull away while still caring deeply. I pretend I'm fine, when I'm anything but.

The truth is... this isn't really about him.

It's about me. It's about my nervous system remembering what it felt like to not feel safe in love. To crave closeness but never be totally sure if it was going to stay. To learn, early on, that sometimes love meant walking on eggshells, or staying busy enough to avoid the ache.

So now, as an adult, even small things can feel big. A short text. A quiet tone. A subtle shift of energy. It sends me back to the part of me that's still waiting to be chosen—fully, consistently, without conditions.

But I'm starting to catch it sooner now.

I ask myself—is this about what's happening right now, or is this an old pattern playing out, again?

Instead of abandoning myself to chase safety, I'm trying to stay.

To breathe through the fear.

To sit beside the version of me who still aches for what she didn't get—and remind her, we're safe now.

I can be what she needed. I can hold her steady, even when everything else feels shaky.

For so long, I thought the answer was someone new.

I left so many people thinking the next person would love me better, love me enough to finally fill that void.

But no one ever could.

No one's love has ever been enough to replace the ache of not feeling wanted by the people who were supposed to want me first.

I've tried—with everything in me—with every man I thought I could love, only to end up running.

But this time, I'm not running.

I'm staying.

I'm doing the work.

I'm finally facing my attachment wounds—without handing them to someone else to fix.

Now that I've uncovered this shadow—the part of me that's been trying to replace a mother's love, to heal abandonment through a man's attention—I can see it clearly.

I didn't realize how deep the void was, or how long I'd been trying to fill it with love from whoever could give me the most.

When it didn't feel like enough, I ran.

I didn't know that kind of emptiness couldn't be filled by someone else.

Now I do.

Now I know that I can fill that space with my own love.

By finding my shadows, tracing them to the root, and untangling the unconscious emotional patterns that have been driving my story—so I can finally love someone for real.

Let them love me back.

Let that be enough.

I'm learning how to forgive people when they hurt me, without abandoning myself—or them.

For so long, forgiveness felt like weakness.

Like letting someone off the hook for wounding me.

So I left instead.

I distanced myself before they had the chance to.

Framed it as strength—protecting my peace, guarding my heart—when deep down, I was scared they'd leave me first.

Scared of feeling unwanted all over again.

Now I'm realizing forgiveness isn't about excusing the hurt.

It's about choosing not to carry the pain any longer.

It's about honoring my own boundaries without closing my heart.

I used to think that staying meant self-betrayal.

I see now that staying—when it's safe, and when I choose it—can be healing.

Love isn't about being perfect.

It's about learning how to repair.

To speak what hurt.

To hold space for imperfection without collapsing into fear.

So I'm learning to forgive, not because others always deserve it—but because I deserve peace.

I'm learning how to stay, not just with them—but with me.

Let's Look at the Emotional + Generalized Attachment Style Breakdown

Core Reflection:

"I distanced myself before they had the chance to... I was scared they'd leave me first. Scared of feeling unwanted all over again."

Pattern Type:

This is a protective survival pattern rooted in fear of abandonment.

Preemptively pulling away may appear as strength or self-respect on the surface, but often it's a deeply conditioned reaction to the threat of emotional loss. The underlying belief may be: If closeness isn't guaranteed, it's safer not to get too close at all.

Core Emotions Involved:

- Fear of abandonment
- Grief over emotional neglect or absence
- Shame around emotional needs
- Loneliness masked as independence
- Resentment disguised as boundary-setting

Attachment Style Patterns at Play:

This behavior reflects traits of disorganized attachment—a mix of anxious and avoidant styles.

- Anxious side: Craves deep connection, fears rejection or being unseen
- Avoidant side: Pulls away when intimacy feels overwhelming or unsafe

When these opposites collide, it becomes difficult to feel safe in closeness or in distance—creating internal chaos. This often traces back to inconsistent caregiving, where the same person may have been both loved and feared, wanted and emotionally unavailable.

Why It Feels Unconscious:

This pattern often forms in early environments where emotional needs were unmet, dismissed, or unreliable.

As a child, shutting down emotionally or withdrawing first may have been the only form of control available in a chaotic or unpredictable relationship dynamic. Over time, these protective instincts become internalized—so much so, they feel like personality traits rather than survival mechanisms.

Shadow Clues:

What This Might Look Like:

- Feeling the urge to disconnect after small emotional triggers
- Pulling away as soon as the connection feels uncertain
- Interpreting quietness or space as a threat
- Ghosting or becoming emotionally distant without a clear explanation
- Suppressing emotional needs to maintain a sense of control
- Telling oneself "I don't care" to avoid vulnerability
- Cutting people off quickly, even if they haven't done anything "wrong"
- Framing withdrawal as strength, but feeling hollow afterward
- Oscillating between craving connection and pushing it away
- Unconsciously rewriting the story to justify walking away, even without clear cause

What This Actually Reveals:

This kind of emotional flight isn't about not caring. It's about caring too much—and not feeling safe in that vulnerability.

When closeness begins to trigger fear, the nervous system may decide it's safer to exit than to risk rejection. Instead of saying, "I'm scared you'll leave," the subconscious says, "I'll leave first." That way, the pain feels more controlled—even though it still hurts.

This is often a remnant of disorganized or avoidant-leaning attachment, rooted in early relationships where love was unpredictable, conditional, or emotionally unsafe.

It can feel empowering in the moment—but it's often a trauma-informed illusion of power, built on fear rather than true emotional sovereignty.

Common Patterns That Arise:

- Becoming cold or unavailable when someone gets too close
- Ending relationships suddenly, especially after feeling emotionally exposed
- Believing that staying is weak, and leaving is strength
  Feeling regret or loneliness after distancing—but not knowing how to return
- Equating emotional independence with protection rather than choice

This is not emotional immaturity—it's a survival strategy.

Often, the body is still trying to protect the self from the original abandonment, not the present situation.

The Beliefs Behind the Pattern:

- "If I get too close, they'll hurt me or leave me."
- "It's safer to end it than to risk being left behind."
- "Needing someone means I'm weak."
- "Vulnerability isn't safe—it's dangerous."

These beliefs form early—often from parents or caregivers who were inconsistent, emotionally unavailable, or left during key developmental years. The nervous system learns that closeness equals risk.

How It Affects the Nervous System:

The fight-or-flight system becomes conditioned to interpret emotional intimacy as a threat. Even a small shift in tone, availability, or presence can trigger a deep, embodied response:

- Heart racing
- Numbness or dissociation
- Sudden need for space
- Irritability or emotional shut down

This isn't about logic—it's a trauma response masquerading as independence.

The nervous system doesn't trust that love can stay, so it prepares to leave before abandonment can happen again. Over time, this creates a cycle of self-protection that reinforces the very disconnection the heart longs to heal.

The next step is learning how to support the nervous system in staying present—even when vulnerability feels unfamiliar. That's how the cycle begins to break.

An example of more Shadow Clues:

"They just didn't love me enough."

What This Might Look Like:

- "I always give more than I get."

- "No matter how much they loved me, it wasn't enough."
- "I left because I didn't feel chosen the way I needed to."
- "They didn't see me the way I needed to be seen."

These phrases may seem like emotional truths on the surface—and in many ways, they are. But often, they also signal the presence of an old attachment wound operating beneath conscious awareness. The wound doesn't speak in logic—it speaks in patterns, unmet needs, and emotional echoes.

What This Actually Reveals:

At the core of this language is an unhealed emotional void—often stemming from childhood experiences where love was inconsistent, conditional, or absent altogether. That absence creates a kind of hunger that doesn't just disappear with time. It hides, waits, and later re-emerges in adult relationships disguised as intensity, urgency, or dissatisfaction.

When love doesn't "feel like enough," what's really happening is that the emotional blueprint from childhood is being reactivated. The adult mind might blame the partner, but the nervous system is still searching for a parent.

This isn't manipulation or self-sabotage. It's survival. The inner child is simply trying to finish a story that was never safely closed.

Common Patterns That Arise:

- Jumping from person to person, hoping someone will finally feel like "home"
- Idealizing new relationships and becoming disillusioned when the initial high fades

- Feeling emotionally starved even in loving, committed partnerships
- Equating emotional intensity with proof of love
- Leaving before being left—or testing others to see if they'll stay

These are not flaws in personality. They are adaptations—creative, desperate ones—that try to protect the self from the deeper pain of feeling emotionally invisible.

The Beliefs Behind the Pattern:

- "If someone truly loved me, I'd finally feel whole."
- "I have to earn love by giving more, doing more, being more."
- "Their love should heal what my parents never could."
- "If it doesn't feel like enough, it must mean I'm not enough."

These beliefs are rarely spoken aloud. They live in the background, shaping behavior and emotional reactions, often without full awareness.

How It Affects the Nervous System:

When early love was unsafe, unpredictable, or conditional, the nervous system learns to stay on high alert—constantly scanning for signs of disconnection or emotional deprivation. Even in moments of calm, the body may anticipate abandonment or disappointment. This can create:

- Chronic tension or anxiety in relationships
- Difficulty relaxing into connection
- Emotional "overreactions" to subtle changes in tone or behavior

- A need to control or manage closeness in order to feel safe

Over time, this leaves the system stuck in cycles of activation and shutdown—reaching out, pulling away, craving love, then running from it. The body doesn't know the difference between then and now. It only knows what has felt dangerous in the past.

Understanding this pattern is the first step. The next is learning how to support the nervous system in unlearning it.

That's where we go next.

The Nervous System and Emotional Survival

Our attachment style isn't just something we think—it's something we feel in our bodies. That's because early emotional experiences get recorded not just in our memories, but in our nervous system.

From birth (and even in the womb), the developing nervous system is constantly scanning for cues of safety or danger in the environment—especially from caregivers. This system, called neuroception, is unconscious. It's part of how the brain learns to predict what will happen next so we can survive.

When caregivers are warm, responsive, and consistent, the child's nervous system learns to stay regulated. Over time, this builds what we call emotional resilience: the ability to handle stress, recover from upset, and stay connected to others during conflict.

However when a child grows up in an environment with unpredictable affection, chronic criticism, emotional withdrawal, or outright trauma, the nervous system does something incredibly adaptive: it begins to treat connection itself as a potential threat.

Here's what that can look like:

- Sympathetic dominance (fight-or-flight): The child becomes hypervigilant, anxious, or emotionally reactive. Their body is always braced for rejection or conflict.
- Dorsal vagal shutdown (freeze): The child emotionally checks out, goes numb, or detaches. They stop expecting comfort or protection and retreat into themselves.
- Fawn response (appease): The child learns to anticipate others' needs, stay agreeable, and suppress their own discomfort to avoid rocking the boat.

Over time, these responses become habitual—automatic pathways in the brain and body that continue firing into adulthood, even when the original danger is long gone.

This is the root of emotional dysregulation: when our reactions to stress, conflict, or intimacy don't match the current situation but instead echo a deeper imprint from childhood. It's not that we're "too sensitive" or "overreacting"—it's that we're responding from a nervous system that was shaped in unsafe conditions.

Reframing the Problem

It's common to feel broken when connection doesn't feel safe—when we cling too hard, shut down too fast, or can't seem to find ease in relationships.

The truth is:

Your nervous system is not malfunctioning—it adapted to protect you.

Understanding this begins to remove the shame. It helps us see our patterns not as flaws, but as intelligent responses to unmet needs. That awareness is the first step toward healing.

While attachment styles describe how we relate to others emotionally, trauma responses describe how our body reacts to threat. They often overlap—but they aren't the same. One is relational; the other is physiological. Together, they shape how we protect ourselves when connection feels risky.

Attachment Healing Chart

Each attachment style carries a unique emotional rhythm, a way the heart has learned to keep itself safe. Healing begins by recognizing the old pattern and learning how to return to presence, self-trust, and authentic connection.

Attachment Style	Description of Healing Path
Secure Attachment	Rooted in emotional balance and trust. Those with secure attachment naturally regulate through safety, connection, and self-awareness. Their healing practices involve maintaining balance: grounding, communication, boundary maintenance, and nurturing consistency in relationships.
Anxious Attachment	Characterized by hypervigilance and fear of abandonment. The path to healing focuses on nervous system soothing, releasing control, and learning self-validation. Practices: breathwork, affirmations of self-worth, compassionate inner dialogue, and gradual exposure to self-soothing when alone.
Avoidant Attachment	Defined by emotional distance and overreliance on independence. Healing begins with softening the walls built around the heart. Practices: somatic grounding,

Attachment Style	Description of Healing Path
	vulnerability exercises, and connecting to safe people while observing discomfort without retreating.
Disorganized Attachment	A blend of approach and retreat, seeking closeness while fearing it. Healing comes through stabilizing the nervous system and repairing trust with the body. Practices: trauma-informed therapy, guided visualization, inner child work, and gentle embodiment rituals that create predictability and self-safety.

The 4 Primary Trauma/Survival Responses (also called "F's"):

1. Fight
    - Activated by the sympathetic nervous system
    - Behavior: controlling, aggressive, confrontational
    - Internal message: "If I can dominate or fix the situation, I'll stay safe."
2. Flight
    - Also sympathetic nervous system

- Behavior: perfectionism, anxiety, overthinking, escapism
- Internal message: "If I move fast enough or stay busy, the danger can't catch me."

3. Freeze
    - Governed by the dorsal vagal branch of the parasympathetic nervous system
    - Behavior: dissociation, numbness, withdrawal, collapse
    - Internal message: "If I shut down completely, I won't feel pain."
4. Fawn
    - A blended or adaptive response
    - Behavior: people-pleasing, hyper-attunement to others' needs, loss of self-identity
    - Internal message: "If I can keep everyone happy, I won't be hurt or abandoned."

Emerging Trauma Responses

→Tend-and-Befriend: Rooted in caregiving as protection

→Submit: Total collapse or resignation in the face of threat

Some experts and somatic therapists now explore "tend-and-befriend" or "submit" as secondary patterns or blended responses, but these are not as widely used in clinical frameworks as the Big Four.

Tend-and-Befriend

What it is:

This response is rooted in relational survival. Instead of fighting, fleeing, freezing, or appeasing, the system responds to stress or threat by nurturing others or seeking connection as a form of protection.

Origin:

Coined by psychologist Shelley Taylor, this theory highlights how, especially in women (biologically and socially), oxytocin may promote bonding behaviors under stress rather than aggression or escape.

What it looks like:

- Trying to calm a chaotic environment by taking care of everyone
- Forming alliances during conflict
- Protecting children or others from danger
- Distracting from the threat by caregiving or creating emotional closeness

Key difference from fawn:

While fawn is rooted in appeasement and fear of disapproval, tend-and-befriend is more about proactive nurturing or connection-seeking in the face of threat. It's less about surrender, more about care as a form of survival.

Submit (Collapse/Appease)

What it is:

This is sometimes considered a deep freeze response or a "submit" reflex seen in both animals and humans when there's no perceived chance of escape or safety.

What it looks like:

- Emotional collapse
- Going along with something unwanted to avoid worse harm
- Emotional numbness while "complying" under pressure
- Feeling powerless, voiceless, or flattened

Rooted in:

The dorsal vagal shutdown system (same as freeze), but even deeper—it's not just about disconnecting, it's about completely submitting to survive.

Think:

"If I stop resisting, maybe I'll get through this alive."

Key difference from fawn:

Fawn still involves action, control, or hope to keep the peace. Submit is shut-down compliance with no real sense of control—it's resignation.

By now, you've seen how the body learns to protect itself when love feels uncertain—through hypervigilance, shutdown, appeasement, or emotional retreat. These aren't flaws; they're survival instincts shaped in childhood and carried quietly into adulthood. But over time, what once kept us safe can start to keep us stuck, especially when these responses begin shaping how we show up in our relationships, our choices, and our sense of self.

Survival Responses Summary

The nervous system protects us through instinctive patterns. Recognizing your dominant response helps you work with it rather than against it.

Fight	Energy surges outward as control, defensiveness, or confrontation. Core emotion: anger masking fear. Healing focus: channel energy into assertiveness, movement, and empowerment without aggression.
Flight	Movement becomes escape. Overthinking, overworking, or restlessness often appear. Healing focus: learning stillness, deep breathing, body awareness, and safe containment of energy.
Freeze	The body shuts down to preserve safety. Numbness, dissociation, or fatigue dominate. Healing focus: gentle reawakening through movement, warmth, breath, and reestablishing connection with the present moment.
Fawn	Safety sought through pleasing and compliance. Boundaries blur to avoid rejection. Healing focus: self-assertion, boundary rituals, journaling unmet

Fight	Energy surges outward as control, defensiveness, or confrontation. Core emotion: anger masking fear. Healing focus: channel energy into assertiveness, movement, and empowerment without aggression.
	needs, and re-learning that disagreement does not equal danger.

Survival Strategies in Unsafe Attachments

When love feels dangerous, we don't stop needing it—we just learn to survive without trusting it.

That survival looks different for everyone. For some, it becomes people-pleasing and perfectionism, trying to be "good enough" to earn connection. For others, it looks like emotional numbing, self-sabotage, or fierce independence anything to avoid the vulnerability that closeness requires.

These aren't random quirks. They're deeply patterned, trauma-informed behaviors—created by a nervous system that learned love might come with a cost.

Below are some of the most common survival strategies born from early attachment wounds:

1. People-Pleasing

Why it forms:

When a child grows up in an environment where love feels conditional—based on behavior, performance, or emotional caretaking—they learn to shape-shift. Their safety depends on others being okay, so they suppress their needs to keep peace.

How it shows up in adulthood:

- Constantly anticipating others' needs
- Difficulty saying "no" or setting boundaries
- Fear of disappointing people
- Identity rooted in being helpful, agreeable, or "easygoing"
- Emotional resentment that never gets voiced

What it's protecting:

People-pleasing is often a survival strategy rooted in anxious attachment. It's a way to prevent rejection by being "good," helpful, and needed.

2. Hyper-Independence

Why it forms:

When early caregivers were unreliable, critical, or emotionally unavailable, the child learns to rely only on themselves. Vulnerability starts to feel unsafe, even dangerous.

How it shows up in adulthood:

- Pride in never needing help
- Distancing when things get emotionally intimate
- Difficulty receiving love, care, or support
- Confusing control with safety
- Feeling suffocated by closeness

What it's protecting:

This strategy is often linked to avoidant or disorganized attachment. It protects the inner child from needing someone who may not show up—or from being disappointed again.

3. Emotional Numbing

Why it forms:

In environments where feelings were invalidated, punished, or overwhelming, the child learns to detach from their emotions altogether. Numbness becomes a shield against feeling too much.

How it shows up in adulthood:

- Disconnection from desires, sadness, or joy
- Feeling "flat" or indifferent even during emotional events
- Over-reliance on distractions (work, food, substances, screens)
- Struggling to cry or express deeper feelings
- Saying "I don't know what I feel" often

What it's protecting:

Numbing is a freeze response, rooted in nervous system shutdown and typically linked to disorganized attachment. It protects the self from emotional overwhelm or disappointment.

4. Self-Sabotage

Why it forms:

When a child internalizes the belief that love, success, or happiness won't last—or that they don't deserve it—they may unconsciously destroy what they crave before it can be taken away.

How it shows up in adulthood:

- Ending healthy relationships out of fear
- Procrastinating or undercutting your own goals
- Creating chaos in moments of peace
- Believing "this is too good to be true"
- Avoiding vulnerability right when things get close

What it's protecting:

Self-sabotage often comes from disorganized attachment—where love was both wanted and feared. The nervous system confuses safety with danger and tries to regain control through destruction.

5. Perfectionism

Why it forms:

When a child feels love is tied to performance—grades, appearance, behavior, or achievements—they may internalize the belief that being "better" makes them safer. Mistakes feel dangerous because imperfection might invite shame, criticism, or rejection.

How it shows up in adulthood:

- Chronic fear of failure or being "found out"
- Overworking, over-achieving, or procrastination due to fear of not doing it perfectly

- Harsh inner critic
- Anxiety over small errors or not meeting expectations
- Difficulty relaxing or celebrating accomplishments

What it's protecting:

Perfectionism is often rooted in anxious or avoidant attachment. It protects the self from shame, disappointment, and the vulnerability of being seen as "not enough." It says: "If I do everything right, maybe I'll finally be safe, wanted, or worthy."

6. Caretaking / Over-functioning

Why it forms:

In homes where emotional chaos, addiction, or neglect were present, a child may become the emotional anchor—taking care of others to feel valued or stay connected. They learn to anticipate needs, solve problems, and manage others' emotions while ignoring their own.

How it shows up in adulthood:

- Taking on others' responsibilities or emotions
- Attracting emotionally dependent or unavailable partners
- Feeling guilty when not helping or fixing Suppressing personal needs to avoid being "too much"
- Resentment when help isn't reciprocated

What it's protecting:

Often tied to anxious attachment, this strategy maintains closeness through usefulness. If you're irreplaceable, you're less likely to be abandoned. It also echoes fawn and tend-and-befriend responses—caring as a form of emotional control.

7. Withdrawal / Shutdown

Why it forms:

When expressing emotions leads to punishment, ridicule, or disappointment, a child learns to disappear. Silence becomes safety. The body numbs, the heart closes, and the inner world becomes a safer place than the outside one.

How it shows up in adulthood:

- Going quiet or emotionally distant during conflict
- Withdrawing when overwhelmed, triggered, or disappointed
- Difficulty expressing emotions in real time Being seen as "cold" or "hard to read"
- Feeling safe only when alone

What it's protecting:

This is often rooted in avoidant or disorganized attachment and freeze-based trauma responses. Withdrawal shields the self from shame, rejection, and the chaos of emotional intimacy.

8. Testing Others

Why it forms:

If caregivers were inconsistent, unavailable, or emotionally unpredictable, a child may grow up doubting whether love is real or stable. As an adult, they may create emotional "tests" to see if someone will stay—mirroring their early experience of uncertainty.

How it shows up in adulthood:

- Pushing people away to see if they'll come back
- Starting arguments to create proof of loyalty
- Overanalyzing small actions or tone changes
- Creating emotional distance and waiting for others to lose the gap
- Secretly fearing being "too much," but still needing constant reassurance

What it's protecting:

Often linked to disorganized or anxious attachment, testing gives the illusion of control in a situation that feels emotionally unsafe. It asks: "Can I trust you to love me, even when I make it hard?"

9. Ghosting / Emotional Detachment

Why it forms:

When closeness felt threatening or emotionally overwhelming in childhood, the nervous system learned to dissociate from connection itself. Emotional detachment becomes a default—not out of cruelty, but out of fear.

How it shows up in adulthood:

- Suddenly cutting people off with no explanation
- Feeling "nothing" in moments that should be emotional
- Avoiding intimacy or commitment when things get serious
- Becoming unreachable during emotional conversations
- Detaching before you can be hurt or exposed

What it's protecting:

This is typically rooted in avoidant or disorganized attachment. Ghosting can be a form of flight or shutdown—a last-ditch attempt to avoid rejection by disappearing first. It's not indifference. It's protection.

✧ Personal Story Prompt:

Think of a time when you pulled away from something good, not because it was wrong, but because it felt unfamiliar, uncertain, or "too much." What might you have been protecting yourself from?

I've lived inside most of these patterns without realizing it. Some seasons, I was the over-functioning caretaker. Other times, I was ghosting people I loved or numbing out just to feel in control. For a long time, I thought they were different problems—but they all traced back to the same wound: I didn't feel safe being seen, wanted, or fully loved. These strategies weren't about who I was. They were about who I had to be to survive what love felt like back then.

The Shadow Side of Love:

When Connection Becomes a Threat

For many of us, love was never just love. It was tension. Confusion. Emotional labor. It meant being needed, not nurtured—being careful, not comforted. So when someone shows up with affection, presence, or care, it doesn't always feel good. Sometimes, it feels terrifying.

This is the shadow side of love: when connection itself becomes the trigger.

We may not realize it consciously, but our nervous system remembers. It remembers the moments when love was unpredictable or conditional. When being close meant being hurt. When being visible meant being judged. When asking for something meant being shamed, ignored, or emotionally abandoned.

So now, even in relationships that seem safe, something in us bristles.

We flinch when someone gets too close.

We shut down when we need to open up.

We test, sabotage, or disappear—not because we don't want love, but because we don't trust it will stay.

Emotional Push-Pull

When attachment wounds go unhealed, it's common to experience push-pull dynamics in close relationships. One moment we crave connection, the next we feel smothered by it. We might long to be chosen, but panic when someone gets too close. We reach for love, then reject it as soon as it arrives.

This isn't an inconsistency. It's trauma logic.

To the nervous system, connection is both the medicine and the threat. The body wants closeness but fears what might come with it: abandonment, rejection, engulfment, and betrayal. So we swing between the parts of us that want to merge and the parts that need to run.

Why We Confuse Intensity with Love

When early love was chaotic or inconsistent, we may begin to equate emotional intensity with emotional truth. We mistake anxiety for chemistry. We assume that love must feel dramatic, consuming, or overwhelming to be real.

So when someone feels calm, grounded, or secure, it might feel... boring. Foreign. Not enough.

This is often the legacy of attachment trauma: it scrambles our internal compass. It tells us that peace is unfamiliar and that safety must be a setup.

When Love Has Strings Attached

In families where love was used to control, manipulate, or punish, it may never have felt unconditional. You might have learned that you had to earn affection, hide your truth to keep the peace, or become what someone else needed you to be.

This creates a pattern where even healthy love feels like a trap. You wait for the other shoe to drop. You hold back pieces of yourself, fearing they'll be too much. Or you disconnect entirely—just to avoid the pain of being seen and still not accepted.

The Heart vs. The Body

One of the hardest parts of healing is realizing that what your heart wants and what your body feels safe receiving are not always the same. You may want closeness, commitment, and intimacy. But if your nervous system has been shaped by relational trauma, those things can trigger panic, shutdown, or deep discomfort.

This isn't because you're broken.

It's because you're protecting something that once needed protecting. Until that part of you feels safe, love will continue to feel like danger—even when it isn't.

Breaking the Cycle — Learning to Feel Safe in Love

Healing from unsafe attachment isn't about becoming perfect in relationships—it's about learning to feel safe in your own body, even when connection feels unfamiliar or uncertain. The goal isn't to eliminate your triggers or erase your past, but to develop the tools and inner safety required to respond with intention instead of reaction.

This section offers practical tools to help you begin that process.

1. Nervous System Regulation: Rewiring for Safety

Your nervous system is your body's security system. If you grew up in an environment where love was unpredictable or threatening, your system likely learned to brace—even in moments that seem calm now. Regulation tools help retrain that response.

Simple Daily Practices for Regulation:

- 5-5-7 Breathing: Inhale for 5 seconds, hold for 5, exhale for 7. Repeat 3–5 rounds to signal safety to your body.
- Orienting: Gently turn your head and slowly scan your environment. Name 5 things you see, 3 things you hear, 1 thing you feel. This grounds you in the present.
- Vagus Nerve Stimulation: Humming, singing, or splashing cold water on your face can activate the parasympathetic nervous system and reduce emotional overwhelm.
- Butterfly Hug (bilateral stimulation): Cross your arms over your chest and alternate gentle taps on your shoulders. This technique helps calm and integrate the brain's emotional response during stress.

2. Grounding Practices: Returning to the Present

When triggered, the body often leaves the moment. Grounding helps bring you back—so you can respond, rather than react.

Grounding Techniques:

- Weighted objects: Use a weighted blanket or press your feet into the floor to anchor your awareness.
- Touchstone object: Carry a small item that represents safety. When triggered, hold it and breathe.
- "I am here" statements: Repeat: I am safe. I am here. This is now, not then.
- Self-contact: Place one hand over your heart, the other over your belly. Breathe slowly and remind yourself: I'm allowed to feel. I'm allowed to stay.

3. Boundaries: Teaching Yourself Safety Through Action

Boundaries aren't just for other people—they're how you teach your nervous system what safe, what's not, and that you will protects yourself when needed.

Types of Boundaries to Practice:

- Physical: Creating space, saying no to touch, honoring your body's cues.
- Emotional: Not over-explaining, not absorbing others' feelings, naming your emotional truth.
- Energetic: Taking space after conflict, limiting time with emotionally draining people, ending conversations that feel unsafe.

Boundary-Building Tools:

- Practice saying no without apology: “No, that doesn’t work for me.” Silence is allowed.
- Notice resentment: Often, chronic resentment is a signal that a boundary has been crossed.
- Tiny boundary practice: Start with low-stakes scenarios (e.g., asking for a different table at a restaurant) to build confidence.

4. Self-Soothing: Becoming the Safe Presence You Needed

In unsafe attachments, we often look to others to regulate our emotions. Healing means learning to offer that regulation to ourselves.

Self-Soothing Techniques:

- Create a comfort corner: A cozy space with calming smells, textures, and lighting where you can go when overwhelmed.
- Write a letter to your younger self: Offer the reassurance and words you needed then, now.
- Sound therapy: Use calming playlists, singing bowls, or tuning forks to bring harmony back into your body.
- Movement: Gentle rocking, stretching, or even dancing can release stored tension and reconnect you to your body.

5. Inner Reparenting: Healing the Source, Not Just the Symptom

Survival strategies often formed in childhood. Reparenting is the process of becoming the loving, consistent presence you didn’t always have.

How to Begin:

- Name the part of you that's scared: "The part of me that panics when I don't get a reply is 7 years old and afraid of being left."
- Respond to that part like a caregiver: "I see you. You're not alone anymore. I'm here now, and we're safe."
- Set routines and care rituals: Make sure your inner child has structure, rest, nourishment, and kindness every day.

6. Pattern Awareness: Naming the Survival Strategy, Interrupting the Loop

We can't change what we don't notice. Becoming aware of your triggers and responses helps you interrupt the loop.

Tools for Pattern Recognition:

- The Pause Practice: Before reacting, ask: What am I feeling? What am I fearing? What do I need?
- Pattern journaling: Track what situations activate you, how you respond, and how it feels after.
- Name the strategy aloud: "This is my anxious attachment showing up." Naming it begins the misidentification process.

7. Affirmations for Attachment Healing

These statements aren't for bypassing pain—they're for re-patterning your inner dialogue in moments of fear or self-doubt.

Try affirming:

- I am allowed to ask for what I need without shame.
- It's safe to be seen.
- I am no longer waiting to be abandoned.
- My worth is not based on how much I give.
- I can trust myself to choose what's right for me.

These tools aren't quick fixes. They're steady practices—tiny acts of returning to yourself, over and over again. Every time you ground your body, honor your limits, or sit with an emotion instead of fleeing it, you're rewriting your nervous system's story. You're not erasing the past—you're teaching your body and your inner child that connection no longer has to feel like a threat. Safety isn't something you have to chase from others anymore. It's something you can build within. From that inner safety, something new begins to bloom.

Reclaiming Your Capacity for Love

When you've spent a lifetime surviving love, opening to it again can feel almost... dangerous.

But there comes a moment—sometimes quiet, sometimes loud—when surviving isn't enough anymore. You begin to long for more than just safety. You start to hunger for connection. For real presence. For love that doesn't make you shrink.

This section is about that turning point.

It's about the version of you that's ready to do more than just heal—the version of you that's ready to receive.

What Reclamation Looks Like:

Reclaiming your capacity for love doesn't mean becoming perfect at relationships. It means becoming safe enough within yourself to:

- Be honest about what you feel
- Express needs without shame
- Allow yourself to be seen
- Let love in without collapsing, clinging, or running

You don't have to unlearn your entire past overnight. You only have to stay with yourself long enough to recognize when the old story tries to play out again—and choose differently.

From Survival to Connection

True connection begins when you stop outsourcing your safety to other people.

That's what earned secure attachment is: the slow, compassionate rebuilding of trust—not just in others, but in yourself.

It's learning to say:

"I can handle heavy feelings."

"I can stay open even when it's uncomfortable."

"I know how to repair, not just retreat."

"I can love without losing myself."

Integration Questions:

You may want to reflect on these as a check-in:

- When do I feel safest in relationships—and what makes that possible?
- Where do I still feel unsafe—and what does that part of me need?
- What kind of love am I ready to receive now, that I wasn't ready for before?
- What does earned safety feel like in my body?

Final Reflection

- There was nothing wrong with you—only a need to protect what was never tended to.
- Every pattern that once protected you was love in disguise.
- But now?
- Now, you get to love yourself enough to stop surviving.
- You get to choose relationships that reflect your healing—not your hurt.
- You get to become the safe place you've been searching for.
- From there—everything changes.

Shadow Sheet

When Love Feels Dangerous

Take your time with these. Let your answers come from the version of you who no longer has to protect, perform, or prove. Just be honest. That's where the real healing begins.

1. When you think about the phrase "love felt dangerous", what memory, person, or feeling comes to mind first?

----

2. Which attachment style(s) felt most familiar as you read this chapter?

Do you notice different patterns show up in different relationships?

----

3. What survival strategy did you learn early on that helped you feel safe or stay connected to others?

What did that strategy protect you from? How has it helped you survive? How is it limiting you now?

----

4. Think of a time when your nervous system responded to a small trigger in a big way.

What do you think your body was remembering in that moment?

----

5. Which trauma response(s) do you tend to default to under stress: fight, flight, freeze, fawn, tend-and-befriend, or submit?

What does that look like for you in real time?

----

6. When do you feel safest in relationships?

What are the qualities or behaviors that help you soften or trust?

----

7. Where do you still feel unsafe in love, intimacy, or connection?

What does that part of you need in order to feel safer?

----

8. What does earned safety look and feel like in your body?

How do you know when you're self-regulated vs. in survival mode?

----

9. Which of the tools in this chapter stood out to you the most?

Which one are you willing to try (or keep trying) as an act of emotional re-parenting?

----

10. What kind of love are you ready to receive now... that you weren't ready for before?

Chapter 6:

THE REPRESSED SELF

"The body keeps the score... but the soul holds the silence."

Section I: The Hidden Cost of Survival

There are parts of ourselves we buried so long ago that we don't even remember digging the hole.

Sometimes it wasn't a single event that caused the burial — it was a slow erosion. A lifetime of being told to "calm down," "get over it," or "be grateful." The world doesn't always need to scream at us for us to lose our voice. Sometimes it only needs to ignore us long enough.

For many of us, the repression of emotion didn't begin with a conscious choice. It began with necessity. As children, we absorb not just the rules of our households but the emotional temperature of our caregivers. We instinctively sense what is safe to express — and what might cost us connection, approval, or peace. So we learn, we adjust, and we internalize.

If anger was punished or ignored, we learned to smile instead of scream.

If sadness was dismissed, we learned to choke it back and power through.

If joy was "too much," we learned to dim ourselves.

If pain made people uncomfortable, we learned to pretend we were okay.

These patterns don't feel like repression at the time — they feel like survival. Like fitting in. Like being "good." We earn love by abandoning pieces of ourselves. Over time, the cost of that transaction gets higher.

As children, survival strategies often look like people-pleasing, silence, staying out of the way, or overachieving. In those early years, it may have meant hiding tears, fixing everyone's moods, or never needing too much. These are not personality traits. They are adaptations. A child will choose disconnection from themselves if that disconnection secures the attachment they rely on to survive.

In adulthood, the same strategies evolve into more complex, often more "socially acceptable" patterns. The child who learned to make herself invisible might grow into the woman who over-accommodates in relationships, tolerates mistreatment, or avoids conflict to the point of self-betrayal. The teen who found worth through achievement may become the adult who ties their entire identity to productivity, constantly striving but never feeling whole. The boy who was told to "man up" might grow into a man who can't cry even when he desperately needs to — not because he doesn't feel, but because he no longer knows how to access the part of himself that does.

Survival looks different when you're no longer a child. It becomes more internal, more disconnected, and harder to recognize. You might have a job, a family, and a to-do list. You might be the go-to person, the caretaker, the calm one in a crisis. On the surface, everything may look fine. Inside, though, you might feel hollow. Like you're performing a version of yourself without ever feeling fully at home in your own body.

That performance is often praised. People admire your strength, your independence, and your work ethic. No one questions the cost. Most don't even know to ask.

These adult survival strategies get rewarded, which is part of what makes them so difficult to examine. You may not even realize that the very behaviors getting you praise are also keeping you emotionally starved. When you're always the one holding space for others, there's often no one holding space for you.

We start to see these behaviors not just as responses to trauma, but as identities we mistakenly believe are us. The strong one. The good girl. The one who never complains. The one who always bounces back. These identities are not our truth. They are armor.

This is where repression hides in plain sight. What once shielded us slowly begins to confine us. The body holds on to what the mind has buried, and the *nervous system carries* the weight of what was *never spoken*.

Repression isn't just a mental process. It's a full-body experience. The feelings we couldn't afford to feel didn't vanish — they sank deeper. Into our muscles. Our posture, our breath, our gut — they all carry the weight of what we go through. Fatigue settles into our bodies, tightness creeps into our muscles, and stomach aches flare up without warning. Thoughts race, emotions go quiet. Some of us stop breathing deeply without even realizing it. Others clench their jaw, hunch their shoulders, or tighten their belly, as if bracing for a danger they can't quite name.

Eventually, the nervous system doesn't know how to downshift. Even in moments of safety, it stays on alert. That's because your body never received the message that it was okay to stop surviving.

Many of us live in a chronic state of overdrive — emotionally, physically, energetically — not because we want to, but because we never learned what rest actually feels like. Safety, slowness, stillness... these things can feel foreign or even dangerous when your entire body is wired to anticipate harm.

We survive by pushing it all down — but survival isn't the same as living.

Healing begins when we stop asking, "What's wrong with me?" and start asking, "What did I have to survive?" This shift matters. It creates space for compassion to enter. It allows us to see our symptoms not as failures, but as brilliant responses to impossible circumstances. The moment we begin to honor the intelligence behind our coping, we unlock the doorway to something deeper: remembrance. Beneath the armor, beneath the exhaustion, beneath the roles we were forced to play — there is someone still intact. That self is not lost. She is waiting. Returning to her is not easy, but it is always possible.

This chapter is about what gets buried, what it costs us to keep it buried, and how we begin the sacred work of remembering and reclaiming what we were told to forget. It begins with permission — not to explain, justify, or rush — but to simply name the truth:

You were never too much.

You were never broken.

You were simply surviving.

Now, we learn what it means to return.

Section II: The Psychology of Repression

Repression is not forgetting. It is forced forgetting — the kind that happens below the surface, without permission or awareness. This kind of forgetting doesn't erase the experience. It buries it, locks it away in the nervous system, and hides it from the conscious mind. Most people don't even realize it is happening.

To understand repression, it helps to distinguish it from two other protective mechanisms: suppression and dissociation. These terms are often used interchangeably, yet each one has a specific function in the psychology of survival.

Suppression is a conscious decision. It happens when a person chooses to avoid a thought or feeling, even if temporarily. Someone might say, "I just can't deal with that right now," or "I'm choosing not to think about it." Suppression delays emotional processing, but it does not erase the memory.

Repression, by contrast, is entirely unconscious. The psyche buries an emotion, a need, or an experience because facing it feels too dangerous, too overwhelming. There's no choice involved — the mind doesn't ask permission. It simply steps in to protect. For a child who grows up with constant fear, invalidation, or neglect, this protection may come at a heavy cost. Not only the memories, but also the feelings tied to them, get locked away. What's hidden stays hidden — until the body, or life itself, insists on bringing it back to the surface.

Dissociation occurs when there is a split between experience and awareness. It can be a temporary break in attention, a foggy sense of time passing, or a complete separation from emotion and bodily sensation. In trauma therapy, dissociation is recognized as one of the most effective

— and exhausting — defenses the nervous system can create. It disconnects us from the unbearable, often leaving us emotionally numb, physically frozen, or energetically scattered.

These three mechanisms — suppression, repression, and dissociation — are not chosen consciously. They emerge in environments where expressing emotions is unsafe or unwelcome. They are adaptations to chronic overwhelm. The child who learns not to cry because it leads to ridicule, or who stops sharing their feelings because they are ignored, is not making a rational decision. That child is being wired for emotional self-erasure.

Children are especially vulnerable to repression because their brains and nervous systems are still developing. They rely on external cues to determine what is okay to feel. When anger is met with punishment, sadness with dismissal, or joy with shame, the child begins to believe that emotions themselves are the problem. The body and brain then work together to silence what was once instinctual. Expression gives way to suppression. Suppression gives way to repression. Over time, a kind of emotional amnesia forms.

In trauma-informed therapy, repression rarely shows up as a neat memory with a tidy resolution. It often emerges through indirect symptoms: chronic anxiety, depression, numbness, fatigue, panic attacks, or the inability to form secure relationships. Clients may say things like, "I don't remember much of my childhood," or "I feel like something happened, but I can't name it." These statements are not gaps in personality. They are signs of protective systems doing their job.

Therapists trained in somatic and trauma recovery models do not rush this process. Repressed material does not need to be dragged into the light. It returns naturally when the body has enough safety, presence, and internal permission to release what was held. This return can take the form of sensations, dreams, sudden tears, discomfort in the chest or gut, or a sense of being "off" without knowing why.

The goal is not to relive trauma. The goal is to integrate what was once too painful to acknowledge. Emotional truth cannot be forced. It can only be welcomed.

Dissociation often accompanies repression. Someone who has spent years compartmentalizing their emotional reality may describe themselves as detached, disconnected, or lost. It can be difficult to access joy, stay present in intimacy, or recall important moments. They may say:

- "It's like I'm watching my life happen from outside myself."
- "I can't feel anything, even when I want to."
- "Whole parts of my memory just feel like fog."

These descriptions are common. They are not evidence of dysfunction. They are signs of a deeply intelligent nervous system that did what it needed to survive.

Over time, dissociation and repression stop protecting us from the world and start protecting us from ourselves. Not only are we numb to pain, but we become numb to wonder, to creativity, to connection. Joy feels unreachable. Desire feels dangerous. Intimacy feels unsafe. This is the cost of long-term emotional disconnection.

Another layer that reinforces repression is shame. Shame is the voice that says, "You're too much." "You're not enough." "You feel that, you're broken." Shame becomes the silent glue that holds repression in place. It makes us fear our own inner world. It teaches us to reject our truth before anyone else has a chance to.

In therapy, shame must be dismantled gently. A client cannot reclaim their repressed parts while believing those parts make them unworthy. Healing begins when the therapist becomes a safe witness to emotions the client once believed were unlovable. In that sacred space, grief can finally breathe. Anger can find expression. Vulnerability becomes a bridge back to selfhood.

Outside the clinical setting, repression shows up in ordinary ways. You may find yourself crying unexpectedly during a movie or commercial. You might overreact to a small inconvenience and feel overwhelmed by your own response. You may avoid certain places, songs, or people without knowing why. These are not signs that something is wrong with you. These are signs that something inside you remembers.

Repression is a silent sculptor of behavior. It shapes the way we connect, the way we parent, the way we cope, and the way we numb. It influences our habits, our careers, our patterns in love. When we are unaware of what lives in the unconscious, it often shows up in our choices.

The good news is this: nothing repressed is gone forever. Emotion is energy. It moves when it is safe to move. You do not need to remember every detail of the past to heal from it. You only need to create space for truth to return — without shame, without urgency, and without the demand for perfection.

There is no expiration date on emotional truth. Even if your story has been hidden for decades, the body holds the key. Healing does not demand that you remember everything at once. It only asks that you begin listening — with patience, with gentleness, and with the courage to believe that what was once buried still matters.

Section III: What We Learn to Swallow

Repression does not always look like silence or avoidance. Often, it looks like responsibility. It looks like being the one who always holds it together. It looks like fixing everything for everyone else, while quietly drowning in the unmet needs of your own.

Many of us learned early that vulnerability had a price. Being sad made people uncomfortable. Being angry made them leave. Needing too much made us feel like we were too much. So we swallowed our truth. We smiled instead. We stepped up. We over-functioned.

This is where repression hides in plain sight.

It shows up as the woman who always has a solution, even while falling apart inside.

It shows up as the mother who gives her children everything she never had, without realizing she is still starving for it herself.

It shows up as the teenager who becomes "the responsible one" after the family falls apart, not because she was ready — but because someone had to be.

As we mature, these behaviors often become fixed identities. We begin to believe we are the roles we play, forgetting that they were born out of survival. These identities can feel natural, even noble. In reality, they are masks for the deeper parts of ourselves we were taught to hide.

The peacemaker keeps everyone happy to avoid conflict. She learned that tension leads to rejection, so she silences her own discomfort to maintain harmony.

The achiever earns approval through perfection and productivity. She learned that his worth is measured by how much she produces or how well she performs.

The caretaker anticipates the needs of others before they are even spoken. She learned that love is something you earn by giving, not something you deserve just by existing.

The comedian lightens the mood to deflect attention away from pain. She learned that humor was safer than honesty.

The chameleon adapts to every environment and relationship. She learned that survival depends on being whoever people want her to be.

Each of these archetypes emerges from an unspoken agreement: "If I become what others need, I will be safe." That agreement keeps us alive in environments where authenticity feels dangerous. Eventually, it becomes exhausting.

We begin to notice that something essential is missing. Even when we succeed, we feel empty. Even when we are praised, we feel unseen. Even when we are surrounded by people, we feel alone. These roles do not make us feel more whole. They make us feel more invisible.

Repression is not always a disappearance of memory. Sometimes it is a disappearance of identity. We forget who we were before we learned to shape-shift. We forget what we want, what we like, what we need. Some of us lose our ability to make decisions without checking how others might react. Others struggle to identify emotions at all, relying on external cues to decide what is acceptable to feel.

This is not a lack of self-awareness. It is evidence of chronic self-abandonment.

One of the most damaging beliefs that lives beneath these roles is this: "If I let people see the real me, they will leave."

That thought is not irrational. It is rooted in experience. Somewhere along the way, authenticity was met with punishment, rejection, or disconnection. So we learned to hide.

The problem is that hiding doesn't end the pain. It delays it. The parts of us we repress do not disappear. They wait. They show up as resentment, burnout, physical illness, anxiety, or emotional numbness. They surface in relationships where we feel used, unseen, or constantly misunderstood. These symptoms are not failures of character. They are invitations to stop abandoning ourselves.

Healing begins with recognition. We must name the roles we've been playing and ask ourselves where they came from. Who did I have to be to survive? What was I taught to suppress to be loved?

For some, the answer is rage. For others, it is joy, neediness, fear, or softness. Repression is deeply personal. No two people swallow the same emotions in the same way. Yet many carry the same ache: "I don't know who I am without these roles."

This question is not a dead end. It is a beginning.

You may recall my own early experiences with caretaking. The way I stayed busy was with soccer, cheerleading, and band after my mother left. The way I threw myself into activity was not because it made me feel strong, but because it kept me from feeling anything else. That busyness was praised. People called me motivated, focused, and goal-driven. Few recognized that you were actually grieving in motion.

Later, as an adult, that same caretaking energy evolved into over-giving in relationships. You became the one others leaned on, the one who held space for everyone else, the one who rarely asked for anything in return. You weren't trying to be a martyr. You were simply repeating what had once kept you emotionally safe.

These patterns did not make you weak. They made you adaptive. They reveal the brilliant ways you learned to survive. Still, they are not your truth.

You are allowed to set them down now.

Reclaiming your repressed self does not mean rejecting the strengths you've developed. It means reconnecting with the parts of you that were left behind in the process. It means learning to honor your needs, express your feelings, and take up space — without apology.

Try asking yourself:

- What part of me have I been pretending not to be?
- What emotion do I judge most in others?
- What would I say if I didn't care who stayed or left?

These questions may not offer quick answers. They will offer direction.

Your roles were never the problem. The problem was believing they were your identity.

You were never meant to live inside a role. You were meant to live inside your truth. The journey back to yourself will not require you to destroy what you built to survive. It will only ask that you stop hiding behind it. Your truth is not too much. It is medicine. Let it speak.

Section IV: When Repression Turns Into Addiction

Addiction didn't begin as recklessness for me. It began as relief.

I didn't think of it that way at the time. In my teenage years, drinking felt like freedom. It gave me space from the pressure I didn't yet know how to name. At first, it was lighthearted — something that made me feel older, braver, a little more in control. It helped me detach from the intensity of what I carried. I didn't recognize it as coping. I thought I was just having fun.

Through my twenties and thirties, drinking was woven into everyday life. It was part of trips, celebrations, cookouts, and girls' nights. I was what many would call "high-functioning." I wasn't missing work, falling apart, or losing things — not yet. I scheduled my drinking around responsibilities. It all looked normal from the outside. It even felt normal for a long time.

What I didn't realize was how deeply tied my drinking had become to my emotional survival. I used it to loosen the grip of the roles I felt stuck inside — the helper, the caretaker, the strong one. I used it to feel something different, or to feel nothing at all. I used it to push emotions further down when I didn't have the energy to face them.

By 2020, everything began to shift. I couldn't deny the patterns anymore. What used to feel like a choice had started to feel like a need. I wasn't drinking to celebrate. I was drinking to disappear. I looked forward to it in ways that felt desperate. I kept telling myself I could cut back, that it wasn't that bad. The truth was harder to hold: I didn't feel okay without it.

That was the year I realized how deeply I had been using alcohol to manage what was unspoken and unresolved. I saw how much I relied on it to cope with overwhelm, exhaustion, and suppressed pain. I saw how the shame around my drinking was layered on top of shame I hadn't yet faced — the shame of feeling too much, needing too much, and never being able to fully relax unless something else helped me let go.

I want to name this clearly for others who may relate: addiction is not always loud or dramatic. Sometimes it's quiet, high-functioning, and socially accepted. It can hide behind roles and responsibilities, behind ambition or caregiving. It doesn't always look like hitting rock bottom. Sometimes it looks like a glass of wine that becomes two, then three, then every night. Sometimes it looks like something you plan your whole day around.

Addiction doesn't always involve substances, either. I've seen how easily repressed emotions get funneled into compulsive behaviors — scrolling, emotional eating, caretaking, cleaning, working, or needing to be in control. These are the kinds of addictions that get praised, not questioned. Overgiving can look like generosity. Overworking can look like ambition. Perfectionism can look like drive. Many of these patterns go unnoticed because they benefit the people around us, while slowly disconnecting us from ourselves.

Each of these behaviors serves a purpose. They give us something — relief, distraction, sedation, structure. They make our lives feel manageable when our inner world feels overwhelming. The more we repress, the more we reach. We reach for anything that will regulate the nervous system, quiet the mind, or numb the pain we don't have words for.

What I've learned through this process is that addiction isn't about weakness or lack of discipline. It's about pain.

Specifically, it's about pain that had no other place to go. When our systems have carried unprocessed grief, rage, loneliness, or trauma for too long, they eventually find a way to release the pressure. For me, that release came in the form of alcohol. For others, it might be food, control, chaos, or caretaking. The core is always the same: the thing we reach for is trying to do what we were never taught to do for ourselves.

Eventually, my nervous system forgot how to regulate without a crutch. I didn't know how to rest, how to be with my feelings, or how to stay in my body through discomfort. Everything felt easier with a drink — until it didn't. Until it started stealing more than it gave. Until it stopped helping and started harming.

The hardest part wasn't putting the glass down. The hardest part was facing everything I had pushed down underneath it. I had to sit with emotions I hadn't touched in years. I had to stop performing the version of myself I thought the world wanted. I had to learn to feel what I used to run from.

Recovery for me has not been linear. There have been moments of deep resistance, grief, and vulnerability. There has also been clarity. There has been a return to truth. I no longer believe healing means perfect sobriety or never struggling. I believe it means becoming more honest with ourselves — about what we feel, what we need, and what we are still afraid to face.

Addiction often mimics connection. It promises comfort, safety, peace. What it actually delivers is isolation. It disconnects us from our bodies, from our emotions, from our relationships, and from our inner knowing. Healing is the process of returning to those things. Not all at once. Not without discomfort. Slowly, consistently, with compassion.

There is no shame in how I coped. There is only gratitude for the self who did what she had to do. She made it possible for me to be here now, writing this. She bought me time. She gave me enough space to survive long enough to begin again.

If you see yourself in any of these patterns, I hope you know this: you're not broken. You're not weak. You're not alone. The fact that you adapted to impossible circumstances does not mean you're damaged. It means you're incredibly resilient. Healing doesn't require you to erase your past. It asks you to tell the truth about it. It asks you to hold space for the version of yourself who didn't have what she needed — and to finally give her the safety she was always searching for.

Section V: How Emotional Repression Shows Up in the Body

Emotional pain that has no outlet doesn't just vanish. It settles into the body.

That's one of the most sobering realizations I've come to through this healing work: the body keeps the score, whether or not we give it permission. I used to believe that if I didn't talk about something, it would eventually stop hurting. If I stayed busy, if I kept pushing through, if I didn't name it — it would dissolve. What I've come to understand is that silence doesn't dissolve pain. It buries it deeper.

The body becomes the storage space for all that goes unspoken. Tension, tightness, migraines, fatigue, stomach issues, panic, numbness — these are not random. They are messengers. They are the signals of truth we haven't yet allowed ourselves to feel.

For years, I experienced unexplained fatigue that would take me out for days at a time. No medical explanation, no obvious trigger — just complete shutdown. I would find myself exhausted to the point of collapse, yet unable to rest. My mind would race, my body would ache, and everything in me would scream for stillness that I didn't know how to give. At the time, I chalked it up to overwork. Now I know it was my body begging me to stop bypassing what needed to be felt.

I was twenty-six when my body gave me a message I couldn't ignore. I was working at a university as the administrative assistant in the academic affairs office. One day, while sitting at my desk, my chest suddenly tightened so severely that I could hardly take a breath. It came out of nowhere. I wasn't anxious. I didn't have asthma. I was simply doing my job, and then, without warning, I could no longer breathe deeply. The pressure in my chest was so intense that I left work and rushed to the doctor, terrified about what might be happening.

They ran X-rays, but everything came back normal. They took bloodwork and told me I'd have to wait for results. A week passed, full of tension and uncertainty. When I finally got called back in, the doctor told me they believed it might be lupus. I was shocked. I knew lupus was serious and came with a lifetime of difficult symptoms. They referred me to a specialist — an hour away — who ran more extensive tests: X-rays of my entire body, multiple rounds of bloodwork, endless questions. The conclusion was that I did have an autoimmune disease, but it wasn't lupus. It was rheumatoid arthritis. It made sense to me at the time. My Mamaw Betty, my dad's mother, had severe arthritis. I thought maybe I had just inherited her condition.

I was placed on medication, tested every three months, and monitored closely. They tried multiple prescriptions — some of which made me sick. One medication triggered an emotional spiral so intense that I ended up in the emergency room, crying uncontrollably and feeling completely out of control. I was referred to pain management therapy. I did what I was told. I followed their protocols. I tried to believe this was just my biology.

One day, the specialist sat me down and asked how stressful my life was. I told him I was working full-time as an administrative assistant, trying to grow a real estate career on the side, raising two kids, and managing everything at home. He looked me straight in the eyes and said, "What's happening in your body shouldn't be showing up until you're in your late forties or fifties. Something in your life is causing this. Your body is responding to stress."

That moment changed me. It was the first time a medical professional connected my illness not to genetics or chance, but to how I was living. To how much I was carrying. To how much I wasn't expressing, asking for, or slowing down to feel. My body had been screaming what I wouldn't say out loud. I had ignored it, overridden it, medicated it — until it refused to be ignored any longer.

I've had panic attacks that didn't feel like fear — they felt like floating. My body would go cold, my chest would tighten, and suddenly I was no longer fully in the room, at least not mentally. It wasn't until much later that I connected this to dissociation. My body had learned to eject me from overwhelming experiences. It was a survival tactic — intelligent, even life-saving — but over time, it kept me disconnected not just from pain, but from joy and intimacy as well.

One of the hardest parts about repression is how invisible it can be. People don't see it when you're dissociating during a conversation, or when your stomach tightens every time your phone rings. They don't see you forgetting entire pieces of a vacation or losing your words in the middle of an argument. They see you functioning. They see you showing up. They don't see the effort it takes to stay in your body.

This is the paradox of emotional repression: it demands that we abandon ourselves to be acceptable to others. Over time, that abandonment takes a toll — physically, mentally, spiritually. Our symptoms become expressions of everything we've been told not to feel. Anxiety is not just about the present moment. Often, it's about suppressed grief or fear that hasn't been given space to move. Chronic illness doesn't always stem from emotion, but in many cases, repressed trauma intensifies symptoms. The nervous system can only hold so much before it starts to signal distress through the body.

Think of how the body responds to danger. The heart rate increases, muscles contract, breathing shortens, and digestion halts. When we're in fight-or-flight, the body prepares for a threat. If that state becomes chronic — not because of external danger, but because of emotional repression — the body doesn't get a chance to reset. Over time, this leads to burnout, autoimmune flares, adrenal fatigue, digestive issues, and chronic tension.

Reading the work of Gabor Maté helped me to put into words what I had already begun to sense in my own experience. His work draws a direct line between trauma, repression, and physical illness. According to Maté, the body does not lie. When we suppress anger, grief, truth, or fear to belong or feel safe, that energy doesn't disappear. It becomes symptoms. It becomes dis-ease. This is not about blame. It's about inquiry. What has your body been trying to tell you that your mind has been trained to ignore?

The first step to healing is listening. Not just to the mind, but to the body's wisdom. My own healing began when I stopped dismissing my symptoms as weakness and started viewing them as signals. Every migraine, every flare, every wave of anxiety became an invitation to turn inward rather than push forward. It wasn't about overanalyzing every sensation. It was about learning to stay — to remain present with discomfort long enough to understand what it needed from me.

Our bodies don't want us to be perfect. They want us to be present. They want us to feel what's real, even when it's messy. That's how regulation begins. That's how trust is rebuilt — not through force, but through relationships. When we begin honoring our body's signals instead of overriding them, we begin to feel safer inside ourselves. That safety is the foundation of every kind of healing.

For many of us, returning to the body requires unlearning. We've been praised for pushing through, for staying strong, for smiling through the ache. We've been taught that sensitivity is weakness, that emotion is irrational, that pain should be hidden. The truth is that sensitivity is intelligence. Emotion is data. Pain is a portal. Our bodies hold the truth that our survival strategies tried to bury. When we start listening, everything begins to shift.

Sometimes this listening happens in quiet ways. I've cried during breathwork for reasons I couldn't name. I've woken up after Reiki or meditation and felt years of weight lifted from my chest. These experiences weren't dramatic. They were sacred. They reminded me that healing doesn't always come through understanding. Sometimes it comes through surrender.

We don't have to wait until our bodies break down to start listening. We can begin now. We can create space for the truth that lives beneath the tension. We can learn to feel again — slowly, gently, in our own time. Healing the relationship between mind and body is not about perfection. It's about reunion.

If your body could speak freely, what would it say? What has it been trying to show you? These questions are not always easy to answer. They require slowness. They require safety. They require trust. That trust is built moment by moment — every time you choose to stay with yourself instead of abandoning what you feel.

Coming back to your body is an act of reclamation. It is how you unlearn silence. It is how you make room for truth. Your symptoms are not betrayals. They are calls for attention. They are proof that what you feel matters, even if no one ever told you so.

The more I've honored the signals in my body, the more I've come to see it not as a battleground, but as an ally. It never stopped trying to communicate. I had just stopped listening. Now, every sensation — even the uncomfortable ones — feels like a form of truth-telling. My body isn't against me. It is for me. It always has been, and so is yours.

Section VI: Dissociation, Disconnection, and The Disowned Self

Dissociation is not always dramatic. Sometimes it looks like zoning out while someone is speaking. Sometimes it feels like driving home and realizing you don't remember the last ten minutes. Other times, it feels like being surrounded by people you love and still feeling completely alone.

For a long time, I didn't know I was dissociating. I just thought I was "really good at staying calm." I believed I had mastered the art of staying composed in the face of chaos. I didn't understand that my body had simply learned to check out. I didn't know that numbness wasn't peace — it was protection.

Dissociation is the mind's way of distancing from what feels unsafe to experience fully. When emotional overwhelm becomes chronic, the psyche learns to create space by separating from sensation, memory, or identity. In trauma work, this is often seen in clients who say, "It's like it happened to someone else," or "I feel like I'm watching my life from outside my body." I've said both.

Disconnection doesn't just happen during traumatic moments. It happens gradually, over time. It happens when you're constantly prioritizing others over yourself. It happens when you feel like you have to perform who you are instead of actually being it. It happens when your truth is silenced, when your needs go unmet, when your body becomes a battlefield instead of a home.

I've experienced this kind of disconnection in ways that were hard to name. I've felt numb during moments that were supposed to be joyful. I've forgotten full chunks of trips or holidays. I've felt like a ghost in my own life — visible, but not fully present.

There is a loneliness that comes with disowning parts of yourself. You begin to feel like a stranger in your own story. You forget what you like. You forget what you need. You forget what you believe. The parts of you that learned to disappear don't just vanish. They wait — beneath the surface — hoping you'll come back for them.

This is the disowned self. The version of you that carries your softness, your anger, your hunger, your creativity. The version of you that stopped showing up because it didn't feel safe to be seen. Dissociation protects, but it also divides. It fractures identity. It creates distance between who you are and who you feel allowed to be.

The first time I started to reclaim my disowned self, I cried without knowing why. The tears weren't about a specific memory. They were about the grief of realizing how long I had been gone. I missed myself. I missed the girl who used to dream, who used to write, who used to feel things deeply before she learned it wasn't safe.

Coming home to the self is not always about finding answers. Sometimes it's about learning how to stay. It's about sitting with the discomfort that used to send you running. It's about breathing into the numbness and waiting for it to speak.

For me, this process included spiritual disconnection too. When I was deep in dissociation, I couldn't feel my intuition. I couldn't hear my inner voice. I felt disconnected from everything — from God, from spirit, from meaning. I questioned whether I had lost my gifts. I hadn't. They had just gone underground, waiting for me to return to my body.

Reconnection starts with presence. It starts with choosing not to abandon yourself, even when everything in you wants to. It starts with learning what it feels like to be in your body without judgment. It starts with naming what's real — I feel numb. I feel lost. I feel like I'm floating. These truths are not problems to fix. They are entry points to healing.

Small rituals helped me come back to myself. Placing a hand on my heart. Meditating, listening to binaural beats, and different frequencies. Journaling without editing. Taking walks without distraction. These practices didn't fix everything, but they helped me remember I was still in there.

Healing from dissociation isn't about going back to who you were. It's about integrating who you've become. The parts of you that went quiet and did so for a reason. They need safety, not shame. They need compassion, not control.

The disowned self isn't broken. She's exiled. She's waiting to be invited back. She holds the key to your vitality, your creativity, your wholeness. Reclaiming her is the work of remembering. It is the work of reunion.

Clinically, dissociation can show up in different ways. Some people experience depersonalization — the feeling of being detached from their own body or self, as though watching their life like a movie. Others feel derealization — where the world around them seems distant, dreamlike, or unreal. In more extreme cases, dissociation can manifest as identity fragmentation, memory loss, or time distortion. Yet even in milder forms, it carries a deep emotional cost. We lose access to our aliveness.

I've had periods of my life that I can barely recall — entire seasons that feel foggy or surreal. I've read old journal entries in my handwriting that feel like they were written by someone else. This is the subtle erosion of self that repression creates. We not only lose memories — we lose the meaning attached to them. We lose the threads that connect us to who we were becoming.

That loss of connection doesn't just impact our memory — it distorts our sense of identity. When I was the most dissociated, I had no idea what I actually liked. I didn't know what I wanted. I deferred decisions to others. I waited for people to tell me what I should feel, or how I should interpret my own experiences. It was as if the compass I had once relied on — my inner truth — had been buried under years of emotional debris.

Rebuilding that connection takes time. For me, it began by noticing the moments I left myself. The phone calls that made my stomach drop. The conversations that made me go quiet. The obligations I said yes to out of guilt. Each of those moments taught me something about my internal system of safety. They showed me where I was still abandoning my truth to protect someone else's comfort.

I started marking those moments with curiosity instead of shame. "There it is again — that floating feeling." "I just dissociated while talking about my childhood." "I can't feel my body right now — why?" These observations became a form of self-study. Not to fix myself, but to understand the architecture of my defense mechanisms.

From that understanding, healing became possible. I learned to pause, breathe, and orient back to my body. I placed my bare feet on the earth. I created small visual anchors in my home — candles, affirmations, crystals — that reminded me to return to the present moment. Over time, my body began to trust that it was safe to stay.

There is also a spiritual dimension to this work. Dissociation doesn't just disconnect us from pain. It severs us from purpose. It clouds our intuition. It dulls our sense of being spiritually held. I used to worry that my spiritual gifts had vanished — my ability to feel energy, to receive guidance, to see auras. In reality, those gifts were still within me. They were simply locked behind a nervous system in survival mode.

As I softened into presence, those abilities began to return. I sensed the presence of my guardian angels. I felt emotional release during Reiki. I began to receive intuitive hits that made no sense logically, yet proved true. Reclaiming the disowned self-opened a channel not just to the body — but to the soul.

We are not meant to live fragmented. Our vitality depends on integration. Wholeness is not perfection. It is permission.

It is the courage to welcome back every part of ourselves — even the ones we had to hide to survive.

If you've ever felt numb when you wanted to cry, distant when you wanted to connect, lost when you wanted to be known — you are not broken. You are protecting something sacred. That part of you that stepped away is not gone. She is waiting for your return.

Section VII: Reclaiming the Truth You Were Told to Hide

Telling the truth after years of repression feels like waking up from a dream you didn't know you were in. The world doesn't look different at first — you do. Your words feel heavier. Your heart beats louder. Your skin becomes more sensitive to the feeling of your own aliveness. The truth was never gone. It was simply waiting for a safe enough space to come forward.

For most of my life, I lived in performance. I learned how to present myself in a way that made other people comfortable. I smiled through heartbreak. I played the role of the strong one. I spoke in ways that made my truth more digestible. My body was holding grief, but my voice didn't say a word. Not because I didn't want to speak, but because I had learned that speaking might cost me love.

Reclaiming the truth you were taught to hide is not a loud or reckless act. It is precise. It is sacred. It is a series of small choices that build a new internal reality. It begins in silence, not shouting. It begins with acknowledging what has been silenced inside of you, not with demanding that others understand it.

The first time I told the truth out loud, it wasn't to someone else. It was in my journal. My hand trembled. My body felt alert. I wrote words I had been thinking for years but had never allowed myself to say. It felt like crossing a threshold. I wasn't just admitting something. I was meeting myself in the rawest way I ever had.

That is how truth begins. In the smallest, most private spaces. A note scribbled in a notebook. A sentence said in a whisper. A memory admitted in the mirror. It doesn't always come out with clarity. Sometimes it arrives messy, half-formed, full of grief. That doesn't make it less valid. It makes it real.

The truths we repress are often the ones we learned were "too much" for others to handle. These truths are rarely about facts. They are about feelings. "I didn't feel safe." "That hurt me more than I let on." "I wasn't okay." These are the confessions that loosen the grip of internalized shame. These are the words that bring breath back into the body.

Reclaiming the truth is not only about the past. It is about the present moment. It is about noticing when you agree to something you don't want. It is about feeling the clench in your stomach when you smile through discomfort. It is about catching the lies you tell yourself in order to keep the peace. Truth doesn't always come in revelations. Sometimes it arrives as self-honesty in real time.

There was a period in my healing when I kept returning to the phrase, "I choose me." At first, it felt foreign. Then it felt selfish. Eventually, it felt like liberation. Choosing myself meant honoring my boundaries, my needs, my timing, my voice. It meant letting go of the people who only knew the version of me that never said no.

The more I told the truth, the more I grieved. I grieved the years I spent silenced. I grieved the relationships built on performance. I grieved the younger me who thought she had to earn her worth by being agreeable, helpful, or invisible. That grief was necessary. It cleared the way for something more honest to take root.

Truth-telling can look like taking up space for the first time. It can look like saying no without apology. It can look like letting yourself cry in front of someone. It can look like disagreeing with someone you love. It can look like leaving the room instead of pretending you're fine. These are spiritual practices. They are not small.

Symbolic rituals helped me reclaim my truth in ways that felt safe and empowering. I wrote unsent letters to the people I had silenced myself for. I burned pages in a fire pit under the moon. I recorded voice notes to my past self, naming what she had survived. These acts weren't about theatrics. They were about returning my voice to its rightful owner: me.

There is a soul-level shift that happens when you begin to tell the truth of who you really are, authentically. It is not just emotional — it is energetic. You begin to call your power back. You begin to feel your intuition rise again. You begin to hear your own voice more clearly than the voices that once told you to stay small.

Reclaiming truth also means releasing the grip of perfection. You won't always say it the "right" way. You won't always find the clearest words. Sometimes your voice will tremble, and sometimes what feels true today will shift tomorrow. That's part of the journey. Truth is not about getting it flawless. It's about finally being free.

Some truths may still feel too raw, too tender, to share out loud — and that's okay. You don't owe anyone the whole story. What you do owe yourself is the honesty of not pretending.

That's where the healing begins: in choosing not to abandon yourself in the moments that matter most.

I've learned to honor the rhythm of my own truth. Some days it rushes through me like a flood; other days it comes as a faint whisper. Both are sacred. Both are enough. What matters is that I no longer silence myself in exchange for love. What matters is that I am shaping a life where my healing doesn't have to be a performance.

Reclaiming the truth you were once told to hide is not a single breakthrough moment. It is an ongoing practice — choosing presence over performance, self-connection over approval, embodiment over erasure. It is the slow, radical act of loving yourself back into wholeness.

Shadow Sheet

I. The Hidden Cost of Survival

What did you have to ignore, suppress, or downplay in order to be "okay" as a child?

What patterns from childhood still show up in your adult relationships?

Who did you have to become to feel safe or accepted?

II. The Psychology of Repression

What emotions feel the hardest for you to access? Why?

Do you notice any parts of yourself you consistently push away or minimize?

How does your body typically respond when you are overwhelmed?

III. What We Learn to Swallow

What beliefs did you internalize about your worth, needs, or voice?

Which archetype(s) do you most relate to: the Peacemaker, the Achiever, the Caretaker, the Ghost?

Complete this shadow statement: "If I told the truth about how I really feel, _____."

IV. When Repression Turns Into Addiction

What behaviors do you turn to when you feel emotionally unsafe or out of control?

Have you ever used caretaking, emotional eating, scrolling, or overworking to avoid your own feelings?

What is the difference between comfort and coping in your life?

V. How Emotional Repression Shows Up in the Body

Has your body ever signaled emotional distress before your mind could recognize it?

What physical symptoms or illnesses have you experienced that might be connected to stress or stored trauma?

How often do you feel fully present and embodied? What supports that presence?

VI. Dissociation, Disconnection, and the Disowned Self

Have you ever felt emotionally numb, disconnected from reality, or like you were "floating" through life?

When do you tend to dissociate or disconnect? What patterns do you notice?

What part of yourself feels most forgotten, exiled, or unseen?

VII. Reclaiming the Truth You Were Told to Hide

What truth have you been most afraid to say out loud?

What rituals or practices help you feel safe enough to speak your truth?

What version of yourself are you ready to reclaim?

Chapter 7:

THE ADDICTED SELF

Addiction is often treated like a personal failure—something we're supposed to fix, hide, or feel ashamed of. But the truth is, addiction usually isn't the start of the problem. It's a sign that something deeper is going on. It shows up when we've been carrying emotional pain for too long, when we feel cut off from ourselves or something bigger, and when escaping becomes the only way we know how to cope.

For some, addiction looks like drinking every day. For others, it might be constant scrolling, taking care of everyone else while ignoring themselves, eating to soothe, or pushing endlessly toward success. These things don't always look like "addiction," especially when the world rewards us for them. Addiction isn't really about how something appears on the outside, it's about what it's doing for us on the inside. It helps numb what hurts. It gives us a way to keep going when staying present feels overwhelming.

This chapter isn't here to label or shame anyone. It is about honesty. It is about pulling back the curtain on the things we turn to when our needs go unmet, our pain is ignored, and our bodies never learn how to feel safe. It's about understanding how we've survived and beginning to see ourselves with compassion, not judgment.

What follows is not a step-by-step guide to getting sober. This is an invitation to tell the truth about what we crave, what we're avoiding, and what it might look like to truly come home to ourselves.

What We Turn to When We're Empty

Addiction is often misunderstood. It is not just about substances or reckless behavior, and it is not only biological. It is a signal, a smoke flare rising from the deeper parts of ourselves that have been silenced for too long. At its root, addiction is a response to pain that has nowhere else to go. It fills the space where unmet needs, buried grief, and spiritual disconnection have taken hold.

I didn't know it then, but I was looking for a way to feel whole. There is a famous story about the beginnings of Alcoholics Anonymous, where the psychiatrist Carl Jung pointed out a strange, beautiful irony: the Latin word for alcohol is spiritus. It's the same word we use for the highest part of our soul. He believed that when we are cut off from our own internal sense of meaning—when we feel that "God-shaped hole" in our chest—we naturally reach for an external "spirit" to fill it. Looking back, I realize I wasn't just chasing a high or a way to relax. I was chasing a connection to myself that I didn't know how to find any other way. I was looking for the spirit I had lost.

Underneath my put-together life, I was thirsty for a version of me that didn't have to perform. I was trying to find a shortcut to the freedom that only comes when you finally stop running.

For many years, I didn't identify as someone who struggled with addiction. I wasn't waking up and reaching for a bottle. I wasn't missing work or facing legal trouble. On the outside, my life seemed fine, put together, even. Underneath it all, there was this quiet, nagging emptiness I couldn't explain.

I kept turning to things that helped me escape wine, relationships, praise, work, not because I didn't know better, but because I didn't know how else to fill the emptiness.

In trauma recovery, there is a question that reframes everything: "It's not about why the addiction—it's about why the pain?" This question invites a softer, more compassionate perspective. It urges us to look beneath the behavior and ask what is crying out underneath it. Addiction isn't a character flaw. It's a trail of breadcrumbs leading us back to the moments where we lost our sense of safety.

Some addictions begin as habits. A drink at the end of a long day. A scroll through social media to unwind. A project to stay busy. These small comforts can quickly become emotional lifelines when we begin to rely on them for the relief we don't know how else to receive. The nervous system, once wired to stay on high alert, will keep chasing what feels familiar even if that familiarity is pain. In that state, numbness can start to feel like the only kind of safety we know.

My own patterns were subtle at first. I convinced myself I was simply unwinding or being social. I didn't yet understand that what I was reaching for wasn't pleasure. It was an absence. I wasn't chasing joy. I was avoiding pain. That distinction matters.

Many forms of addiction don't get labeled as such because they are praised or normalized by society. Overworking is often seen as ambition. People-pleasing is mistaken for kindness. Control is framed as discipline. These patterns can be just as compulsive and just as damaging. They rob us of presence. They keep us in performance mode. They prevent us from listening to what we actually need.

Achievement became one of my earliest addictions. I found safety in being impressive, in being helpful, in being needed. These roles were rewarded, so I clung to them. I believed that if I could stay busy enough, successful enough, selfless enough, I could outrun the feeling of emptiness that trailed behind me like a shadow. It never worked for long.

What I have come to understand is that addiction thrives in the places we feel most powerless. It steps in when we feel disconnected from ourselves, from others, or from something greater than us. Spiritual disconnection is rarely named in "recovery work," yet it is essential. When we lose our sense of purpose, when we forget that our lives are meaningful, we become vulnerable to anything that offers even a temporary illusion of solace.

Addiction is clever. It mimics a connection. It offers the illusion of comfort, belonging, or control. Whether it's through substances, relationships, or workaholism, it tricks the nervous system into believing we are safe—at least for a moment. That temporary relief can become intoxicating, especially for those of us who never learned how to regulate our emotional states.

Some people turn to alcohol. Others to sex, shopping, food, or caretaking. What matters less than the object of addiction is the function it serves. Ask yourself: What does this behavior allow me to avoid? What feeling do I not want to touch? What truth am I trying not to see? These questions do not shame. They reveal.

In the communities I work with, and in the mirror I face, I've seen how addiction often begins with a simple desire to feel better. No one sets out to destroy their life. Most of us are trying to manage what feels unmanageable. We are trying to breathe in spaces that taught us to hold it all in. We are trying to feel in families or cultures that told us not to.

When I reflect on the moments I felt most lost in addiction—not necessarily to substances, but to the illusion of being fine—I recognize a deep loneliness beneath it. That loneliness wasn't about being alone. It was about feeling invisible. It was about carrying emotions no one knew I had because I had trained myself not to show them.

True recovery begins when we stop trying to fix ourselves and start listening to ourselves. It begins when we realize that the thing we are chasing will never fill the place inside us that needs to be held, not escaped. It begins when we stop labeling our coping mechanisms as failures and start tracing them back to the pain that birthed them.

That pain often runs deeper and further back than we realize. Sometimes, we're trying to numb wounds that aren't even ours to begin with. Cultural expectations, unspoken family grief, and the weight of generational silence can shape our patterns just as much as our own lived experiences.

Addiction doesn't always come from big, obvious trauma, the kind with a capital "T." Sometimes, it grows out of the slow, steady ache of being emotionally overlooked. The quiet ways we learn to disappear. The loneliness of never feeling fully seen for who we really are.

In my healing, I had to reckon with all of this. I had to let go of the fantasy that one more goal, one more glass of wine, one more compliment, and one more relationship would finally make me feel whole. I had to sit with the void I had been trying to fill and let it speak.

That is what this section asks of you—not to judge your behaviors, but to become curious about them. Not to shame your patterns, but to listen to their origins. You are not weak for having found ways to cope. You are wise for surviving. Now the invitation is to do more than survive. The invitation is to understand what you've been running from and, gently, when you are ready, turn toward it.

Addiction as Disconnection

Disconnection isn't always loud or dramatic. Sometimes, it shows up as a quiet numbness, gaps in our memory, or a constant low-level sense that something just isn't right. For many of us, addiction begins with this kind of subtle drift—not just away from others, but away from ourselves.

I used to think addiction was about needing more. More wine. More attention. More control. What I've come to understand is that addiction was actually about something missing. I wasn't seeking excess. I was trying to fill a void. I didn't know how disconnected I had become from my own body, intuition, and truth. I only knew that without something to take the edge off, life felt unbearable.

There is a question that reframes this entire struggle, one often asked by healers like Dr. Gabor Maté: "The question is not why the addiction, but why the pain?" When I first heard that, it felt like an exhale I'd been holding for decades. It meant that my patterns—the wine, the people-pleasing, the need to be impressive—weren't signs that I was broken. They were signs that I had been hurting. I realized that my addiction was actually a brave, desperate attempt by my younger self to solve a problem of suffering. It was a survival strategy I created in the moments when the truth of my life felt unmanageable. When we stop trying to "fix" the behavior and start tending to the wound that birthed it, the shame finally begins to dissolve.

For me, one of those wounds was emotional caretaking. I learned early on that my worth was tied to being helpful, kind, and easy to be around. What looked like people-pleasing wasn't just my personality; it was a trauma response. It was how I stayed safe when love felt unpredictable.

When I was drinking socially, it never seemed like a problem. A glass of wine after work. A few drinks on the weekend. Nothing out of the ordinary. What made it dangerous was how it made me feel—confident, calm, relaxed, and less anxious. Alcohol didn't just ease the tension. It silenced the noise. It dulled the parts of me that carried grief, guilt, responsibility, and fear. It made me feel like I could breathe again.

That temporary calm became something I longed for. Eventually, I noticed that I couldn't get through a week without reaching for it. Then it was hard to get through the day. I would tell myself I deserved a break. I would promise to cut back next week. I would try and fail. I started to feel sick almost every day, emotionally and physically. The hangovers became more than headaches. They came with shame, depression, and a deep sense of spiritual emptiness.

During that time, I felt like I had lost my willpower. I couldn't understand why I kept returning to something that made me feel worse. The truth is, I didn't yet have another way to feel safe. I hadn't learned how to sit with myself without a buffer. My body didn't feel like home. My thoughts raced constantly. I felt like a burden, not only to others, but to myself. That's when I began to realize this wasn't about alcohol anymore. This was about disconnection.

Addiction doesn't always look like substance use. Sometimes, it shows up in quieter, softer ways, the kind that settle into the nervous system without us even noticing.

For me, one of those ways was emotional caretaking. I felt like it was my job to manage other people's feelings, especially my mother's. I learned early on that my worth was tied to being helpful, kind, and easy to be around. Over time, that belief turned into a compulsion to keep the peace, even if it meant putting my own needs last.

What looked like people-pleasing wasn't just part of my personality. It was a trauma response, a way to stay safe when love felt unpredictable. This belief became a compulsion. I would sacrifice my own needs to maintain harmony.

I internalized the belief that if I wasn't good, I wouldn't be loved. That belief bled into every area of my life. I became addicted to being needed, to being approved of, to being in control.

Toxic relationships mirrored this pattern. I found myself in two physically abusive marriages. These relationships were chaotic, painful, and deeply familiar. I stayed longer than I should have. I tried to fix what wasn't mine to fix. The emotional highs and lows became addictive. I confused intensity with connection. I convinced myself that if I just loved harder, everything would get better. That never happened.

These patterns were all different shapes of the same wound—disconnection from self. I was so tuned into other people's needs, moods, and expectations that I couldn't hear my own. I ignored the red flags, silenced my intuition, and betrayed myself in small ways every day. Addiction thrives in this kind of environment. It grows where we've abandoned ourselves.

The turning point came during one of the most grief-heavy seasons of my life. I hadn't fully processed the loss of my mamaw, whose presence had been an anchor. Then my mother disowned me again, reopening a wound I had worked so hard to close. Not long after, my granny passed away. I felt emotionally gutted. I tried to quit drinking during this time and couldn't. That's when I knew I had a deeper issue. It wasn't about the alcohol anymore. It was about my inability to feel and function without it.

Healing didn't happen overnight. It took over two years for me to fully stop drinking. During that time, I stumbled constantly. I journaled, cried, wrote poems, meditated, and distanced myself from toxic environments. I didn't have all the answers. I just knew I didn't want to live in disconnection anymore.

Addiction is not just a behavior. It is a signal that something essential has gone missing—our voice, our sense of safety, our spiritual roots. Disconnection from self is often the first wound. Everything else grows from there.

There's a lie that often lives underneath addiction. For me, that lie was: "I only feel like myself when I'm drinking. I can actually think more clearly—once I've had a glass, it calms me down." This belief didn't come from nowhere. It came from years of unregulated anxiety, unresolved trauma, and the false sense of peace I had learned to associate with alcohol. It was only in hindsight that I realized the person I felt like when I was drinking wasn't the real me. She was the version of me who didn't have to feel anything.

True healing meant confronting that lie. It meant facing the parts of me that felt unworthy, anxious, or inadequate without a crutch. It meant learning to be with myself—fully, compassionately, and sober.

Addiction, in all its forms, is a kind of self-abandonment. Whether through substances, relationships, achievement, or approval-seeking, it asks us to trade authenticity for survival. Healing is the process of coming back. It is a return to presence, even when that presence feels raw or terrifying.

What helps is not perfection. What helps is compassion. Curiosity. A willingness to listen to the parts of ourselves we once tried to silence. Recovery is not a straight line. It is a spiral. We return again and again to the places we once left behind. This time, we come with love.

Family, Culture, and the Inheritance of Numbing

Addiction is rarely born in isolation. It is shaped, inherited, modeled, and even praised in the environments where we grow up. Families don't need to talk openly about numbing for the message to be passed down. It lives in what gets ignored. It survives in the silences, the dismissals, and the rewards given for staying strong. Many of us never learned how to feel because we were raised in spaces where emotions were considered inconvenient. Vulnerability was not punished outright—it was simply not allowed.

In my family, strength was the currency. Productivity was proof that you were okay. Emotional needs were kept quiet or hidden entirely. No one told me directly not to cry. I just learned that people didn't know what to do when I did. I watched how the women in my life kept moving, even when they were in pain. I absorbed the lesson early: if something hurts, work harder. Stay busy. Prove you're fine. Pain was something to be powered through, not processed.

That legacy of silence lives in the body. It lives in the tight jaw, the held breath, the smile you keep on your face when your heart is breaking. It lives in the discomfort you feel when someone asks how you're really doing. Even now, I sometimes struggle to answer honestly. Not because I want to lie, but because I was trained to make things easier for everyone else. That's how I kept belonging. That's how I earned love—by not needing too much of it.

Numbing wasn't just something I learned. It was something that surrounded me. I watched adults cope with stress through humor, anger, alcohol, or avoidance. No one called it addiction. No one named it trauma. It was just life. You got up, did what needed doing, and didn't talk about what it cost. That was the script. That was the inheritance.

I carried that same script into adulthood. When I started drinking more regularly, it didn't feel like rebellion. It felt like a release. I had internalized the belief that everyone needed something to take the edge off. A glass of wine after work was normal. It was even a sign of success—something grown, tired women did to relax. It wasn't until I tried to stop that I realized how deeply I had come to rely on it.

I often think about a famous study called "Rat Park" that completely changed how we understand this struggle. Researchers found that if you put a rat in a small, empty, lonely cage with a bottle of drugged water, the rat will drink it until it dies. But if you create a "Rat Park"—a beautiful space with grass, toys, and other rats to connect with—they almost never touch the drugs. They don't need to numb themselves because their environment feels safe and full. Looking back, I realize that the culture I grew up in was a kind of cage. It was a place that valued "hustle" over heart and "performance" over presence. We don't reach for these things because we are weak; we reach for them because we are "social animals" trying to survive in a world that has traded connection for consumption. We were just trying to find a way to breathe inside the cage.

Even now, I see how addiction hides behind cultural approval. The "wine mom" jokes. The hustle culture memes. The praise for women who never rest. We don't just learn to escape ourselves—we are applauded for it.

Culture reinforced the same messages my family had. Pain was personal, not collective. Healing was individual, not communal. Being overwhelmed was expected. Self-neglect was noble. Mothers were expected to sacrifice themselves. Women were told to be everything to everyone. Emotions were framed as weakness. Dependence was shameful. Over giving was admirable. These messages didn't just shape how I saw myself. They shaped what I believed I had to become.

Even now, I see how addiction hides behind cultural approval. The "wine mom" jokes. The hustle culture memes. The praise for women who never rest. The silence around what it costs us to stay so composed. Numbing is baked into the culture we live in. It is made to look beautiful. Marketable. Desirable. We don't just learn to escape ourselves—we are applauded for it.

There is a cost to that applause. It teaches us to measure our worth by how much we can handle. It keeps us in roles that look strong but feel suffocating. It makes us believe that any crack in the surface is a sign of failure. That belief keeps us silent. It keeps us suffering. It keeps us seeking solace in things that hurt us.

I was never taught that my body could be a place of safety. I was never shown how to regulate fear or grief. I was not given language for sadness, resentment, or overwhelm. These were feelings to hide or apologize for. When those feelings got too loud, I did what I had learned to do—whatever it took to turn the volume down.

Addiction, for me, was not a sudden event. It was a slow drift away from myself. It was the inevitable result of a life spent chasing approval, avoiding conflict, and keeping pain out of sight. I didn't grow up around obvious addiction. Yet I inherited it in other forms—in the tendency to disappear emotionally, in the need to be useful, in the belief that survival meant self-sacrifice.

One of the hardest parts of healing has been unlearning the idea that strength means silence. I have had to teach myself how to speak what hurts, how to ask for help, how to stay in my body when everything in me wants to leave. I have had to rewire my nervous system to stop seeing stillness as a threat. I have had to make peace with the truth that I do not owe anyone my composure.

Our culture does not teach us to feel. It teaches us to perform. It teaches us to push through. It teaches us to market our wellness while hiding our pain. That disconnect creates a perfect storm for addiction. Not just to substances, but to roles, identities, personas, and routines that mask our exhaustion.

I have learned that true strength lives in softness. It lives in the trembling voice that tells the truth. It lives in the moment you let yourself cry in front of someone. It lives in the decision to stop running, even if no one else understands. That kind of strength is not flashy. It is not loud. It is not always celebrated. Yet it is the kind that saves lives.

There is grief in waking up. There is grief in naming what was never spoken aloud. There is grief in seeing how much you lost while trying to be who you were taught to be. That grief is transformational. It is not something to be avoided. It is something to be honored.

Healing means telling a different story. It means permitting ourselves to feel what no one else has room for. It means reclaiming the parts of us that were silenced by culture, dismissed by family, or buried under expectation. It means naming the ways we were taught to numb—and choosing, little by little, to come back to life.

Rewriting the Script – From Coping to Connection

There came a point when I realized I wasn't trying to get better; I was just trying not to fall apart. I didn't know what healing was supposed to look like, but I knew I couldn't keep living in survival mode. Everything felt like too much. Also, not enough. I wanted out of my patterns, yet they were the only ones I knew. So I clung to them. I drank to calm my nerves. I performed to feel valuable. I stayed busy to feel important. I disappeared into caretaking, perfectionism, and being the one who "always bounces back."

Deep down, I wasn't bouncing. I was breaking. Quietly. Slowly. Over time.

No one tells you that healing starts in the weirdest places—in your car after another emotional hangover, staring out the window like your skin doesn't fit. In the journal entry, you don't want to write because you already know what it will say. In the silence you used to run from, now asked to sit down and finally listen.

When I first tried to quit drinking, I didn't want sobriety—I wanted peace. I wanted to stop waking up with shame in my stomach. I wanted to stop needing a glass of wine to feel like myself. I wanted to stop lying to myself that I was "just tired" when really, I was empty. Letting go of the bottle also meant letting go of the buffer. I didn't realize how many parts of me I'd been using alcohol to avoid.

Alcohol wasn't the only thing. It was everything I'd used to avoid stillness.

- Over giving until I resented everyone around me
- Saying yes when my body was screaming no
- Chasing praise like it was oxygen

I thought these actions made me lovable. In truth, they were just distractions from a deeper truth I wasn't ready to face: I didn't trust that who I really was—without the roles, the achievements, or the coping—was enough.

That was the beginning of the rewrite.

Not some magical morning where I "chose myself."

It was slower. Messier. Unimpressive.

It looked like crying on the floor, scribbling curses into a notebook.

It looked like meditating with my hand on my heart, whispering "you're safe" even when I didn't believe it.

It looked like unfollowing people who triggered me and saying no without explaining myself.

It looked like sitting in a bath, feeling nothing, and doing it anyway.

The more I slowed down, the louder the truth became.

What I'd been calling strength was actually shutdown.

What I'd been calling coping was actually dissociation.

What I'd been calling independence was actually fear.

Healing didn't come through a program or a guru. It arrived in a slow series of returns—

- Writing poems that made me sob
- Reiki sessions that cleared the noise
- Breathwork that helped me stay in my body
- Letting my spirit speak when my mouth couldn't

That's how I learned the difference between survival and connection.

Survival is what you do to stay numb.

Connection is what you do to feel safe enough not to.

These days, when something triggers me—when I want to scroll, shop, drink, or over-explain—I try to pause. Even just for a moment. I ask myself, What are you trying not to feel right now?

Sometimes I don't even have words for it. Sometimes the ache is ancient. Sometimes it's just sadness that doesn't have a name. Rather than run, I breathe. I light a candle. I sit with it. I write to it.

Healing hasn't made me perfect. It's made me present.

Presence is harder.

Numbing is easy. Scrolling is easy. Powering through is easy.

Still, presence is where the real shift happens.

You don't heal by force.

You heal by listening.

By staying.

By refusing to abandon yourself just because the feeling is uncomfortable.

This is what it means to rewrite the script—not by erasing what you've done to survive, but by honoring the wisdom in those choices, and choosing differently when you're ready. There is no need to hate the old version of yourself. She kept you alive. She was doing her best.

Now is your chance to show her how it feels to be free.

Tools and Practices for Reconnection

Healing didn't come to me in one big breakthrough; it came in fragments—small, quiet moments where I chose to stay instead of escape. I used to think I needed more willpower, but I actually just needed more safety. Jung believed that the only way to truly overcome an addiction was to replace the "false spirit" of numbing with a "true spirit" of connection. These tools are the ways I began to create that true connection, one layer at a time.

This isn't a list of rules. It's a collection of invitations. Try what resonates. Leave what doesn't. Healing isn't about forcing change. It's about offering yourself something different than what hurt you.

1. *Grounding and Getting Back Into My Body*

When I was deep in disconnection, my body didn't feel like home. My thoughts would race, my chest would tighten, and I'd feel like I was floating outside of myself. I didn't know back then that this was a trauma response. I just knew I didn't feel safe in stillness.

Learning to ground myself was the first step in interrupting those old cycles. Some days it looked like placing my hand on my heart and taking a few deep breaths until the shaking slowed. At other times, I had to literally step outside barefoot and put my feet on the earth. Breathing in, breathing out, and telling myself, *you're here. You're safe now.*

These tiny acts of presence helped rewire my nervous system. Not overnight, but slowly, with practice, I stopped needing the glass of wine, the distraction, or the numbness quite as urgently.

2. *Writing the Truth — Even When It Hurt*

Journaling became my lifeline. Not the pretty kind. Not the "dear diary" kind. I'm talking about messy, tear-stained pages that held things I couldn't say out loud.

I wrote to the younger me. I wrote to the part of me that didn't want to feel anymore. I wrote poems that cracked me open. I wasn't writing to fix anything—I was writing to finally tell the truth.

Some of my most powerful reflections came from questions like:

- What am I trying to escape right now?

- What do I need that I'm afraid to ask for?
- Where am I abandoning myself today?

Writing helped me name the grief I'd inherited and the roles I was tired of playing. It helped me stop pretending I was fine.

3. Energy Work and Sound Healing

Reiki taught me that I didn't have to force healing. I could invite it. I could let it flow. I started practicing Holy Fire Reiki on myself in quiet moments, especially when the anxiety was loud or the shame felt heavy. Laying my hands on my heart or my belly became a ritual of return.

Sound healing—using crystal bowls, tuning forks, or even just soft music in the background—helped me move energy that I didn't have words for. These practices didn't erase the pain, but they softened the edges. They helped me feel held when I didn't know how to hold myself.

I started trusting that healing doesn't always come through talking. Sometimes it comes through vibration, through frequency, through stillness.

4. Boundaries That Made Space for Healing

One of the most important things I did during my recovery was remove myself from environments that made me feel like I had to perform, over give, or explain my pain.

Saying no got easier when I realized my nervous system wasn't built to carry other people's chaos anymore. I stopped pretending I could drink "just one" when I knew what would happen. I stopped accepting relationships that cost me my peace.

Setting boundaries wasn't just about protecting my energy. It was about creating space to hear myself again.

5. Reparenting the Parts I Used to Shame

The more I healed, the more I met younger versions of myself—the scared girl who learned to earn love by staying quiet, the teenager who thought alcohol was freedom, the adult who thought being strong meant never needing help.

I started talking to those parts. Sometimes out loud. Sometimes on the page. I'd say, I've got you now. You don't have to hold it all anymore. Reparenting wasn't about fixing myself. It was about learning to stay with myself—especially when I was hurting.

That's the real work: not becoming someone new, but showing up for the parts of you who never had anyone stay.

Healing isn't a straight path. It loops. It circles. Some days I still feel the pull to disappear. The difference now is—I notice it. I pause. I ask, What do you need right now that's actually going to help?

You don't have to be perfect. You don't have to get it right every time. You just have to stay curious. You just have to keep choosing presence over performance—again and again.

Even when it's messy.

Even when it hurts.

Especially when it hurts.

That's how we come back to ourselves.

There were so many days I didn't think I could do this. So many times I swore I was fine while quietly falling apart. Letting go of the things that numbed me felt like losing a lifeline—until I realized those lifelines were also what kept me from truly living. Addiction didn't make me weak. It pointed to all the places I was still trying to survive. That's what this chapter was always about—not the coping, but the coming back. Back to my body. Back to my truth. Back to the parts of me I used to run from. If you're here now, reading this, then you've already started that return, too. And no matter how many times you've left yourself, you can always come back.

Shadow Sheet

The Addicted Self

1. What behaviors, substances, or roles have you used to escape pain or avoid presence?
   (List anything that comes to mind, even if it doesn't "look" like addiction.)

   ----

2. When you reach for those things, what are you usually feeling just before?
   (Loneliness, overwhelm, anxiety, emptiness? Try to name the emotion underneath the urge.)

   ----

3. What were you taught—directly or indirectly—about emotions growing up?
   Were you allowed to feel?
   Were you expected to be strong, quiet, and helpful?

   ----

4. Who did you learn your coping patterns from?
(Think about your caregivers, extended family, or culture at large. What did they model?)

----

5. Which version of yourself did addiction (in any form) help you avoid?
(Is there a younger, softer, angrier, or more vulnerable part of you that was easier to numb?)

----

6. What belief lived under your addiction?
(Examples: "I'm too much," "I have to be in control," "If I stop, I'll fall apart." What felt true in those moments?)

----

7. What practices, boundaries, or moments have helped you reconnect with yourself—even briefly?
(Name anything: journaling, breathwork, walking outside, crying without apology, saying no.)

----

8. What does "coming back to yourself" feel like in your body?
(Describe it in physical terms—warmth in your chest, tears, stillness, etc.)

----

9. What do you want to say to the version of you who was just trying to survive?
(Write a letter or a few sentences. Speak to them like someone you love.)

----

10. What is one thing you can offer yourself now that you didn't know how to give before?
(It doesn't have to be big—just something real. A pause. A breath. A moment of honesty.)

Chapter 8:

THE INNER CHILD ISN'T WHO YOU THINK SHE IS

The Fantasy of the Inner Child

When people talk about healing their "inner child," they often imagine a small, wounded version of themselves—soft, innocent, and easy to love. It's a comforting image. Neat. Gentle. Clean.

But for many of us, the real inner child doesn't look like that. She's messier. More complicated.

She's not just the sweet, abandoned part of you that you want to protect. She's also the one who got in trouble for crying too loudly. The one who was sent to her room for getting angry. The one who learned to perform just to feel accepted, or who buried her needs so deep she can't even find them now.

She might feel ashamed when you try to connect with her. She might not trust you yet. She might still be stuck in the same old story you've been trying so hard to move on from.

Healing your inner child isn't about returning to some perfect version of innocence. It's about coming back to the parts of yourself you were told to hide—the ones that were too emotional, too needy, too angry, too scared. The parts that never had a chance to grow, because no one ever truly saw them.

This chapter isn't here to help you imagine your younger self and send her light. It's here to help you meet her as she really is—and to stop asking her to be someone who's easy to love.

The Inner Child Myth

You've probably pictured her during a meditation: a soft, quiet version of yourself as a child. Maybe she's sitting alone, maybe she's waiting for someone to come back. You imagine wrapping her in warmth, whispering that she's safe now. For a moment, maybe she is.

That version of your inner child, the one you comfort and protect in your mind, is usually only part of the story.

The rest of her might not be so still. She could be yelling. She might be pushing people away. Or maybe she's hiding somewhere deep in your mind, in the places you don't like to go, waiting for you to love her again.

We're taught to view the inner child as someone passive and powerless but she's not. She's alive. She's reactive. She remembers. She shows up in your life all the time, when you panic after being ignored, when you feel small after being criticized, when you shut down in the face of someone else's disappointment.

The myth of the inner child as a symbol of purity or innocence can actually become another way to avoid doing the deeper work. It lets us imagine her as someone fragile and in need of protection, instead of someone who might still carry rage, fear, or shame. It's easier to love the version of her who just wants a hug. It's harder to face the one who's been banging on the walls of your adult life, begging you to stop pretending.

This isn't just about healing the part of you that was wounded. It's about facing the part of you that was silenced. The part that was told she was too much. The part that had to grow up too fast, or the part that never got to grow up at all.

To truly heal your inner child, you don't need to rescue her—you need to see her. All of her. Not just the parts that make you feel tender or sad, but the parts that make you uncomfortable. The ones that make you cringe. The ones that still show up when you're overwhelmed, triggered, or secretly convinced that no one is coming to help.

That's who this chapter is for the version of you that never really left. The little one still tugging at your sleeve, the one you're trying to snatch the balloon from, saying: "Grow up." "Stop being so emotionally immature." But she never went away. She's still waiting—not for you to push her aside, but for you to kneel down, look her in the eyes, and finally listen.

Fractured Selves and Emotional Time Travel

When you experience something painful or overwhelming as a child, your brain doesn't always process it the way an adult's brain would. You don't have the language to make sense of what's happening, or the safety to express it, or the power to change it. Instead, your nervous system finds a way to store the experience. To tuck it away somewhere in your body or mind so you can keep going.

But tucked away doesn't mean forgotten. It means fragmented.

This is why so many of us end up feeling like we're made of different selves. There's the version of you who shows up to work or school or social settings and plays the part—organized, helpful, competent. Then there's the version of you who spirals over a text that goes unanswered, or gets reactive when you feel judged, or shuts down during conflict without knowing why.

These aren't mood swings. They're younger parts of you and when they take over, it's like your adult self disappears and your body starts time-traveling—back to a moment when you didn't feel safe, seen, or in control.

Psychologists call this an "emotional flashback." It doesn't come with vivid images or specific memories, the way a PTSD flashback might. Instead, it comes with feelings: panic, helplessness, shame, rage, and confusion. You suddenly feel small or lost or terrified—and even if you know nothing dangerous is happening, your body doesn't believe you.

This is what unresolved childhood trauma can look like: not a movie reel of the past playing in your mind, but a sudden and overwhelming shift in how you feel right now. A flood of emotion that seems to have no cause—until you realize you've been pulled into a younger version of yourself without even knowing it.

Most people don't recognize when this is happening. They just think something is wrong with them. "Why am I overreacting?"

"Why can't I get over this?"

"Why do I keep falling apart?"

The truth is, there's nothing wrong with you. You're not falling apart—you're remembering. Not in your head, but in your body. In your nervous system. In the parts of you that had to survive something too big to fully process at the time.

When you were little, you may have learned to dissociate—mentally check out, numb your emotions, or pretend things didn't hurt. That protective mechanism helped you get through it. But now, those same parts of you are still trying to protect you, even when the threat is gone.

They don't know you're safe now.

They don't know you're an adult.

They still think you're stuck.

Until you learn how to recognize, regulate, and re-integrate these parts of yourself, you'll keep getting pulled back in time—reacting from a place that no longer matches your current reality.

Healing isn't about deleting those parts. It's about bringing them home. It's about learning how to stay with yourself—even when those younger selves show up in pain, confusion, or fear. Not silencing them. Not shaming them. Just staying.

That's where the repair begins.

The Roles We Inherited as Children

When children aren't given the emotional safety to be their full selves, they don't just shrink—they adapt. They become whatever they think they need to be to stay connected, accepted, or safe. These adaptations don't go away just because we grow up.

Instead, they harden into identities.

Maybe you became "the good girl." The quiet one. The helper. The one who never caused problems, never made a fuss, always did what was expected. Maybe you learned early on that being liked meant being small. Being safe meant being silent.

Or maybe you became the rebel. The loud one. The wild one. Not because you didn't care—but because deep down, you cared too much and had no safe place to put it.

Some people grew up being the responsible ones. They looked after younger siblings, managed the emotions in the house, and learned to read the room like their safety depended on it.

Others learned to disappear. They kept their needs quiet, stayed out of the way, and hoped that if they didn't take up too much space, they wouldn't get hurt.

These are the roles we inherited before we ever had language for them. They were survival strategies, not choices. Often, we wore them so well that we forgot they were costumes. But inside each role is a story of what was missing.

The helper who was never helped.

The good girl who was never allowed to be messy.

The overachiever who was terrified of being unworthy.

The invisible one who longed to be seen.

These roles gave us a sense of control in environments that felt unpredictable or unsafe. Now, as adults, they often keep us stuck in patterns that no longer serve us.

We overgive. Over-function. Over-apologize. We try to earn love instead of receiving it. We ignore our own needs because we were taught they were burdensome. We abandon ourselves in the name of peace.

And beneath it all?

The inner child is still waiting.

Not for praise. Not for perfection.

But for permission.

To be real. To be seen. To be something other than what she had to become.

The Rage and Grief Beneath the Surface

Most people expect their inner child to be sad. What they're not prepared for is her rage.

It's easier to feel sorry for the little girl who was neglected, overlooked, or unloved. But what about the one who's furious?

The one who wants to scream, slam doors, break things, or cry until someone finally listens? The one who's tired of being the nice girl, the strong girl, the understanding one?

That part of you doesn't always get welcomed in healing spaces. She's too loud. Too much. Too unpredictable. So we bury her deeper. We call her dramatic. We try to fix her instead of hearing her. But her rage is a signal. It says, Something was wrong. Something mattered. Something hurt.

The longer we avoid her, the more she shows up in sneaky ways—sarcasm, shutdowns, passive-aggressive comments, uncontrollable panic, sudden outbursts. Or worse, she turns that rage inward. Self-criticism. Shame spirals. Chronic tension. Autoimmune flare-ups. She doesn't disappear. She finds another way to speak.

Right next to her is grief.

Not just grief for what happened, but for what didn't happen.

The moments of comfort that never came. The softness you never got to rest into. The childhood you thought everyone else had. The family memories you only saw in movies. The safety you didn't even know you were missing until it was too late.

This grief doesn't always feel like sadness. Sometimes it feels like emptiness, or jealousy, or emotional numbness. Sometimes it's the ache that rises when you witness someone else being loved the way you needed to be and you can't stop comparing. Sometimes it hits you years later, when you finally feel safe enough to look back and see how unsafe it really was.

Grief is a portal. Rage is a compass. Together, they lead you back to the parts of yourself that never got to feel in real time. The parts that had to armor up too soon. The parts that still wait for someone to say, "You didn't imagine it. It wasn't your fault. It should've been different."

You don't need to fix your inner child.

You need to listen to her.

You need to give her space to feel the things she wasn't allowed to feel.

You need to stop minimizing her pain just because it's inconvenient or loud.

This is the work of reparenting: not just protecting the inner child from the world—but protecting her from you. From your inner critic, from your impulse to silence her again. From your fear of what she'll say if you let her speak freely.

Because once you let her rage...

Once you let her grieve...

She stops fighting you.

She starts trusting you and that's when the real healing begins.

Meeting Her With Compassion, Not Control

When people begin inner child work, they often bring their adult mindset into the process. They want to understand her, fix her, or get her to stop sabotaging things. It becomes another self-improvement project—another attempt to control the parts of themselves that feel unpredictable or uncomfortable.

That's not compassion. That's management.

If your inner child still believes she's only safe when she performs, she won't fully trust your love. If she senses that your attention comes with conditions—"I'll love you when you're calm," "I'll listen to you when you're soft," "I'll accept you when you're done being so emotional"—she'll stay hidden. She's learned what it means to mask for safety, she knows when love is earned instead of given.

True inner child healing begins when you stop asking her to change and start asking her what she needs.

This work doesn't ask you to be perfect. It asks you to be present. Especially when your younger parts feel messy, angry, emotional, or shut down. Those are the moments she needs you most—not the version of you who's trying to talk her out of her feelings, but the version who can sit beside her and say, "I see you. I hear you. You don't have to be anything other than what you are right now."

For many people, this is the hardest part. Not because they're unwilling but because they never had that kind of presence modeled for them. You might have grown up in a home where emotions were shut down, ignored, or punished.

So now, when your inner child starts to speak up, your adult self might react the way your caregivers once did, with avoidance, frustration, or pulling away emotionally.

That doesn't make you a bad person. It means you were never shown how to hold space for yourself in pain. Now, you have the opportunity to learn.

You can become the adult who stays. The one who doesn't flinch at the crying or retreat when the fear shows up. The one who brings softness, not silence. Consistency, not criticism. Presence, not pressure.

This is not about reprogramming your inner child to be easier to live with. This is about reintroducing her to safety—for real this time. Because once she feels safe, she doesn't have to act out. She doesn't have to panic. She doesn't have to pretend.

She gets to rest.

She gets to grow.

She gets to become someone you never had the chance to be.

Integration and Repair

Your inner child doesn't need a rescue mission. She needs a relationship with YOU.

Healing is not about getting rid of her or transforming her into a more polished version of you. It's about integration—learning how to bring her with you, without letting her run the show. She was never meant to lead your life. That job belongs to your adult self. The one with tools. The one with perspective. The one who can create safety where there used to be fear.

Integration begins with simply noticing.

When you feel triggered, overwhelmed, abandoned, or suddenly afraid, try to pause. Ask yourself, *"How old do I feel right now?"*

Chances are, the answer won't match your actual age. You might feel five. Or twelve. Or like the version of you who just found out that love could disappear without warning.

That's your signal. Not a flaw. Not a failure. Just a part of you asking to be seen.

Once you can recognize her presence, you can begin to respond. Create rituals of connection. Set aside quiet moments to check in with your inner child. Use journaling, visualization, or even drawing to bring her voice forward. Ask her what she's afraid of. Ask her what she needs. Ask her what no one ever thought to ask.

Then listen.

When she says she's scared, don't correct her. When she says she's angry, don't dismiss her. When she says she wants to hide, don't force her to come out. Meet her exactly where she is, without pressure. Healing happens in the relationship—not in the results.

Repair takes time. Especially if your inner child is used to being ignored, minimized, or shamed. You'll have to prove your presence through consistency. She won't believe you at first. She's seen promises break before. So keep showing up. Speak to her kindly. Set gentle boundaries when needed. Let her know your adult self is in charge now—and that she doesn't have to protect you anymore.

You may need more than self-talk. Your body holds these patterns too. Co-regulation is key. That might mean breathing exercises, grounding techniques, or simply placing a hand on your heart and saying, "You're safe now." It might mean sitting outside in the sun, feeling the earth beneath your feet, and reminding your nervous system that it's not trapped anymore.

Reparenting isn't about erasing the past. It's about repairing the connection between your younger self and your present self. It's about becoming the caregiver you never had—reliable, compassionate, steady. The one who doesn't leave when things get hard.

Over time, your inner child will stop reacting with panic or fear. She'll begin to soften. She'll trust your presence. She'll feel your care in every choice you make—for your body, your boundaries, your rest, your joy.

That's how healing becomes real. Not all at once. Not perfectly. But day by day, breath by breath, you begin to live as someone whole.

Shadow Sheet

Reconnecting With the Real Inner Child

Use these prompts to explore your relationship with the parts of yourself that were shaped in childhood. Let this be a space of honesty, not perfection. You don't need to censor or analyze your answers. Let whatever rises, rise.

1. What role did you play in your family growing up? Think about how you tried to earn love, avoid conflict, or keep the peace. What did you have to suppress in order to play that role?

   ----

2. When you get emotionally triggered or overwhelmed, how old do you feel in those moments?

   ----

3. Describe what those younger parts of you are afraid of. What do they believe is about to happen?

   ----

4. What parts of your inner child still feel too "messy," "needy," or "unlovable" to face?

----

5. Be honest. Which emotions or traits do you still try to silence or manage in yourself?

----

6. What do you imagine your inner child is still grieving?

----

7. This could be something concrete (a loss, a moment, a relationship) or something vague (a feeling you never got to experience).

----

8. What does your inner child need from you now, as the adult?

----

9. Not a perfect version of you. Not a savior. Just someone who stays. What could that look like?

----

10. What would it feel like to stop performing and just be with yourself?

----

11. What fears come up when you imagine letting go of the "role" you've always played?
What would it mean to offer safety instead of control to your inner child?

----

12. How might you start responding with presence, even when it's uncomfortable?

Journaling prompt:

"Dear younger me, I've been trying to fix you for a long time.... Maybe now it's time to meet you where you are... Here's what I want you to know..."

Chapter 9:

THE GRIEVING SELF

"Grief isn't something you finish. It's a profound unraveling that begins by disorienting you. Over time, it transforms into something you carry, and remarkably, you continue to live. Not because the pain vanishes, but because you discover a new version of yourself, permanently altered by the experience."

When the Ache Stays (intro)

By now, you already know what grief feels like. You've carried it through the pages of this book. You've felt it in the silence after love goes missing, in the ache of not being chosen, in the years you spent pretending it didn't hurt. This chapter isn't where grief begins—it's where we finally stop apologizing for it.

Grief has been here all along, threaded through your memories, buried under survival, waiting for the right moment to be named. You may have called it depression. You may have called it anxiety, fatigue, or failure. You may not have called it anything at all—just tried to outrun it.

You've made it this far. That means something inside you knows it's time. Time to honor what was lost, what was never given, and what had to be left behind just to make it through. This isn't about wallowing. It's about telling the truth. It's about letting yourself mourn the things the world told you to get over.

This chapter isn't a side note. It's a turning point.

Grief isn't new to you. You've carried it for a long time. But now, you're strong enough to face it head-on, without looking away.

No more shrinking it. No more stuffing it down. Your grief deserves to be honored, not hidden.

You've grieved in silence. You've grieved through strength. Now it's time to grieve on purpose.

The Unseen Grief

Some grief is easy to recognize. It shows up with funerals, sympathy cards, and casseroles.

But other grief goes unseen. It hides behind strength. It lives in the stories we rarely say out loud.

The hardest kind to name is the grief that doesn't come from losing something, but from never having it at all.

We're taught that grief belongs to death, to obvious loss. But the deeper I went into my own healing, the more I started to see how much grief I had been carrying all along.

Grief for things I didn't even know I was allowed to miss.

The love that never felt safe. The childhood I had to perform my way through. The parts of me I left behind just to make it through.

That kind of grief doesn't make noise. It settles in. It lives in your body. In your nervous system.

It shows up in the way your stomach tightens when someone gets too close. Or the way you go blank when someone asks how you're really doing.

You might not have called it grief. Maybe you just thought you were tired. Or too sensitive. Or just not yourself.

But that's what it is. It's grief.

Maybe you've been mourning in silence for years—apologizing for your needs, shrinking your truth, pretending you were fine because that's what was expected. Maybe no one told you that what you went through deserved to be grieved. I'm telling you now: it does.

This isn't about blaming the past. It's about giving the pain a name. Grief rises when your body finally believes its safe enough to feel what it couldn't before. That's not a breakdown. That's healing.

The Grief That Follows Her Home

Healing your inner child is not just a sweet reunion. It's a reckoning. When you truly meet her, the girl you used to be, you don't just reconnect. You grieve.

You grieve for what she went through. For how long she had to carry it. For how much she needed and never received. The grief that surfaces in this part of healing doesn't come from a single moment—it comes from years of silence, of being unseen, of learning to shrink to survive.

This is the part where the ache starts to speak. Where your adult self realizes how long you've been pretending not to need.

Let it come. This is not a detour. This is what happens when love finally meets truth.

There's a younger version of you who still remembers what it felt like to go without. She doesn't need to be fixed. She needs to be held. She needs you to stop brushing it off. She needs to know her hurt is real and worthy of care.

This isn't about getting over it. It's about finally turning toward it. With tenderness. With truth. With the kind of honesty that doesn't need to be explained.

Let this be the place where you stop pretending it didn't matter. Let this be where you say it out loud. Grief doesn't always come from what was taken. Sometimes it comes from finally seeing what was missing.

In the early stages of inner child work, it is common to feel hopeful or curious. Many people expect a sense of lightness—like reconnecting with something innocent and lost. Yet what often follows that initial reconnection is not relief. It is grief.

This grief does not come out of nowhere. It arises because meeting the inner child means remembering what she needed but never received. Her unmet needs were not small. They were foundational: safety, comfort, protection, attunement, encouragement. When those needs go unmet, a child does not simply forget. She adapts. She performs. She internalizes the message that her needs are either too much or not important.

As an adult, finally recognizing that truth can be disorienting. You begin to feel the weight of everything you once minimized. You grieve the absence of nurturing, the absence of safety, and the absence of being truly seen. You may have spent years excusing the people who hurt you, rationalizing their behavior, or numbing your pain. Inner child work strips away those defenses. What surfaces is the raw awareness that what happened was not okay.

This grief is not just emotional. It is physical. It often lives in the body long before it is named. You might feel exhausted, unmotivated, tearful, or emotionally raw after doing this work. Some people describe it as feeling "too much," while others feel nothing at all—just a deep ache they cannot explain. These are all normal responses.

Grief also arises from what psychologists call developmental mourning—the sorrow of realizing you did not get the emotional development you were entitled to. This includes grieving the version of you that never got to play freely, speak openly, or trust fully. It is a mourning of potential. Not just who you were, but who you might have become if your emotional needs had been honored from the beginning.

This experience is almost universal in shadow work. It does not mean you are broken or regressing. It means your nervous system is finally safe enough to feel what was once unbearable. Many people try to skip this part of the process, thinking that awareness alone should be enough to heal. In reality, grief is the bridge between recognition and integration. It allows you to stop spiritualizing or intellectualizing your pain and start honoring it.

There is no set timeline for how long this grief will last. Some waves pass quickly. Others revisit for years in new forms. Each return is not a failure but an invitation. You are being asked to witness a new layer of yourself with more compassion than before.

This part of the journey is not glamorous. It will not always feel profound or transformative in the moment. More often, it will feel like heaviness, like fatigue, like an ache you can't quite name. That is not a sign to turn back. It is a sign that you are finally feeling what the younger you was never allowed to feel.

You are not grieving to stay stuck. You are grieving to become free.

You've already met her.

In the last chapter, you began reconnecting with your inner child—not just as a concept, but as a living part of you that still remembers what it felt like to be small, vulnerable, and unheard. For many, that process brings a surge of tenderness or clarity. You might have felt a deep sense of reunion. You might have even felt proud of yourself for finally reaching toward that younger version you had to leave behind.

And then, something unexpected happens.

Instead of lightness, you begin to feel heavy. Instead of peace, you feel unsettled. That ache rising in your chest, the sudden irritability, the wave of sadness you can't explain, these aren't signs you're doing something wrong. They're signs that your body is beginning to grieve.

That's what happened to me.

I didn't expect to feel so shattered after doing inner child work. I thought the hard part would be over once I reconnected with her. But the grief that followed hit me like a wave I didn't see coming. I grieved for everything I never received—the emotional presence I needed, the comfort I silently begged for, the conversations I wish someone had initiated before I made choices that reshaped my life. I started to realize how many mistakes I made not because I was reckless, but because I was emotionally abandoned. I didn't know myself, because no one ever truly took the time to know me.

That realization nearly brought me to my knees.

I cried for the girl I could have been. For the versions of myself I betrayed trying to earn love. For the shame I carried that never belonged to me. I grieved the kind of mother I had wanted to be and the kind of mother I couldn't fully be while still carrying so much unprocessed pain. That grief was quiet but devastating. It stripped away every excuse I had wrapped around myself just to keep going.

Still, it gave me something else too.

It gave me clarity. It gave me grace. I started to understand that this grief wasn't a failure it was a sign that healing had finally begun. Because when you allow yourself to mourn what you didn't receive, you create space for something new to grow in its place. Compassion. Truth. Self-responsibility. Forgiveness.

You can't go back and rewrite your childhood. You can't undo the ways your pain touched others. But you can be honest about it now. You can stop pretending you weren't impacted. You can choose to show up differently from here on out.

This part of healing is quiet. Most people will never understand the weight of it. They will never know what it's like to grieve a mother who is still alive, or to grieve the parent you were while you were still learning how to hold your own pain. They won't see it as grief, but you will. You'll feel it in your chest. In your voice. In the way you start showing up for yourself—softer, slower, with a kind of reverence that wasn't there before.

If you're here, you're not just doing this for yourself. You're doing it for every person who never got the chance. You're learning how to hold space for a kind of grief that rarely gets named.

That is brave.

Let the ache speak. Let it move through. Let it change you. Then take a breath because there are many faces of grief, and this is only one.

The Many Faces of Grief

Grief doesn't always look like tears. Sometimes it looks like overworking. Sometimes it looks like emotional numbness, misplaced anger, or that constant feeling of anxiety you can't shake.

It's easy to miss grief when no one taught you to recognize it. If you learned early on to downplay your pain, chances are you've been grieving in plain sight for years without realizing it.

- There are so many forms of grief we don't talk about. So many names we never give it. We think grief is reserved for funerals, but what about:
- The grief of being emotionally abandoned by a parent who was physically present?
- The grief of not being protected when you needed someone to step in?
- The grief of being the strong one for so long that nobody even thought to ask if you were okay?

These experiences are valid. They count. They stay with us.

Some of this is known as disenfranchised grief—the kind that isn't recognized or validated by the world around you. Nobody sends flowers for it. There's no "grief leave" for growing up too fast. No eulogy for losing a version of yourself you were never allowed to be.

For me, it showed up in layers. The older I got, the more it began to unfold. I grieved the childhood I spent walking on eggshells. I grieved the girl who smiled through things that were tearing her apart. I grieved the years I lost in relationships that drained me, simply because I didn't know how to ask for more. I even grieved the woman I thought I had to become—the one who kept it all together, no matter the cost.

Another form is anticipatory grief—the ache of loss before it even happens. I carried that for years in relationships with people I loved but couldn't trust to stay. I kept bracing for abandonment, because I had learned that closeness always came with a timer.

There's also identity grief—the mourning that happens when you outgrow who you had to be to survive. That one hurts in ways that are hard to explain. It's not just sadness. It's disorientation. You start to realize you don't want to hustle for love anymore, or pretend to be the easygoing one, or keep swallowing your truth to avoid conflict... yet letting go of that version of yourself feels like a death. In many ways, it is.

Grief can also come from emotional inheritance—the unspoken grief passed down through generations. You may have watched your mother suppress her tears or your grandmother power through her pain. You may have been taught that grief is a luxury, that survival leaves no room for softness. As a result, you learned to stay quiet. To cope without complaining. To push through without pause. The grief built up inside you like a storm with no release.

There is no one right way to grieve. Some people cry. Others shut down. Some swing between rage and numbness by the hour.

Whatever your version looks like, it matters. Your grief is not too small. It is not too dramatic. It is not too much.

Grief is personal. It doesn't need a witness to be real. What it does need is your presence. Your willingness to stop minimizing what you've lost. Not everything has to be justified in order to be honored. Some of the most life-shaping losses are the ones we never felt safe enough to name.

If you're feeling disoriented right now, like parts of you are unraveling, know this—you're not doing it wrong. You're grieving. *You're learning how to stop carrying what was never yours.* You're learning to lay it down, piece by piece, and say: This mattered. I mattered.

No one taught us how to do this. We're learning anyway.

Grief Buried in the Body

Some grief never got a voice, so it found a home in the body instead.

It settled in your shoulders, your jaw, your chest. It showed up in the tightness you can't stretch away, in the lump in your throat that rises for no clear reason, in the fatigue that lingers even after a full night's sleep. These aren't just stress signals. They are stories—unspoken sorrow finding shape through sensation.

You may have already explored how trauma lives in the body, though grief speaks its own language. It tends to be heavier, slower, and more tender. It creeps in when we pause. It stirs when we finally feel safe enough to exhale. Many of us never learned to expect grief to show up in physical form, so we didn't know what to call it. The body remembered long before we did.

Grief can show up as:

- A sudden wave of emotion during stillness or meditation
- A hollow ache in your chest when you see someone else receive what you never got
- An unexplained sadness that surfaces with certain smells, songs, or seasons
- The reflex to hold your breath in moments of tenderness

Crying is one way grief moves, though not the only way. Numbness, fatigue, disconnection, restlessness—these are all forms it can take when left unspoken for too long.

When I began doing deeper healing work, my body started grieving before my mind caught up. I would cry out of nowhere, feel exhausted for no reason, or get overwhelmed by sensations I didn't understand. At first, I tried to explain it away. I told myself I was just tired or stressed. In reality, I was finally feeling what I had pushed aside for years.

Grief doesn't always need a clear storyline. Sometimes it's layered, carried over years of unacknowledged sorrow. Sometimes it belongs to the girl who smiled through heartbreak. Sometimes it belongs to the version of you who stayed strong, not because you wanted to, but because being soft wasn't an option.

The body doesn't need us to understand everything it's holding. It needs us to slow down. To listen. To stop pushing the grief away and instead create space for it to move.

You don't have to pry it out or force it forward. You simply have to allow it to rise.

Let the tension soften. Let the tears come, even if you don't know why. Let yourself grieve in the way your body has been asking for all along.

This isn't you falling apart. This is you finally letting go.

Cultural and Family Inheritance of Grief

Some of the grief you carry never belonged to you but you've felt it all the same.

It lingers beneath the surface. You don't always know where it came from, only that it feels heavy... like sadness with no storyline. Like pressure in your chest that doesn't go away. Like tired that sleep can't fix.

This is inherited grief. It gets passed down in silence. Through generations of women who never had the space, the safety, or the support to feel their own heartbreak—who stuffed it, ignored it, and kept pushing through. Whether they meant to or not, they handed it down to us.

You may have come from a family where nobody talked about emotions. Where you were told to be strong, not soft. Where vulnerability wasn't welcome, and asking for what you needed made you "too much." In those homes, grief doesn't get witnessed. It gets absorbed.

The women in my family were tough. Loving, hardworking, loyal—but tough. Not the kind of tough that comes from confidence. The kind that comes from holding everything in. I watched the women who raised me push through physical pain, heartache, abandonment, even abuse and barely speak a word about it. They didn't cry. They didn't complain. They just kept going.

I used to think that was a strength. That belief doesn't live in me anymore.

What they carried didn't disappear. It sank. Into their bodies. Into their relationships. Into their children. Into me.

That's how generational grief works. It hides inside the patterns. The ways we shut down. The ways we lash out. The way we smile when something hurts is because that's what we were taught to do.

If you've ever felt grief that didn't make sense, or emotions that seemed too big for what was happening—this might be why. You may be grieving for things you never got a chance to name. You may be grieving for the versions of your mother or grandmother who never got to be whole. You may be the first person in your family line who's ever had the time, the tools, or the courage to feel this.

That's not something to hide. That's the beginning of healing.

You are the one breaking the cycle. You are the one saying: This ends with me.

This kind of grief isn't just emotional—it's cultural. Many of us were raised with the same messages:

- Don't be dramatic.
- Stop crying.
- Be strong for everyone else.
- Don't make a scene.

We were taught to toughen up. To tone it down. To keep it quiet. Somewhere along the way, we started to believe that our grief was a problem that it made us unstable or selfish or ungrateful.

None of that is true.

Grief is not a weakness to hide. It's a truth trying to come home.

You are not broken for feeling it. You are healing what no one before you had the chance to touch.

Maybe you've always been the emotional one. The sensitive one. The one who felt everything too deeply and asked too many questions. You're not too much. You're the one who felt what no one else would name.

Let that be your medicine. Let that be your strength.

You're not just grieving for yourself. You're grieving for the women who came before you. The ones who held it all in. The ones who never got to say, "This hurts." The ones who never stopped to ask, "What do I need," because no one ever asked them that either.

Grief is not the end of your story. It's the threshold.

Every time you let yourself feel what they could not, you help set them free, too.

Ritual, Release, and Reverence

Grief doesn't move on command. It moves when it's ready. Sometimes it stays silent for years, then pours out in the middle of doing dishes. Sometimes it asks for stillness. Other times, it needs movement, sound, or ceremony. You'll know it when it comes because it won't ask for permission.

By now, you've met some of your own grief. You've felt it in your body, in your memories and in the pieces of yourself you've had to let go of. The question now is: how do you hold it? How do you honor it, instead of stuffing it down again?

Ritual doesn't fix grief, but it gives it somewhere to go.

There's no right way to do this. The most powerful rituals are the ones that feel honest. Not polished. Not spiritual for the sake of being spiritual. Just real.

Let the Words Out

Grief holds a lot of unsaid things. Write the letter. Say the thing. Let the younger version of you speak. Let the goodbye rise if it needs to. Even if you never send it, even if you never read it again, getting it out of your body matters. You don't owe anyone closure but you might owe it to yourself.

Move What's Been Stuck

Your body already knows how to release. Trust it. Cry, shake, stretch, scream into a pillow, punch a mattress, walk until your legs say stop. Don't worry about looking wild. Grief doesn't care how you look—it just wants you to stop holding it in.

Create a Place to Honor It

If it feels right, build a space. Light a candle. Place something meaningful on a shelf or altar—a photo, a note, a dried flower, a symbol. Not to be dramatic. To be intentional. To say: This mattered. You don't need a reason. You don't need approval. This is your grief. Let it be sacred.

Name What You Lost

You already know that not all grief comes from death. Some of it comes from what you never got. The love that didn't arrive. The version of yourself you had to leave behind. The trust that was broken. The mother who couldn't mother. Give yourself space to name it. Speak it out loud. Write it down. Draw it if words won't come. If it hurts, it counts. If it changed you, it deserves to be honored.

Let It Come in Layers

You've seen by now that grief doesn't follow a clean arc. It loops, it lingers, it returns. That's not backsliding. That's depth. A new layer is surfacing. Stay with it. Each wave is a chance to meet yourself with more presence than the last time.

There's no need to force a ritual. Choose what feels true for you. If all you can do today is light a candle or place your hand over your heart and breathe—that's enough.

Make space for what's real. Give it breath. Give it form. Give it the reverence it's always deserved.

No one in my family lit candles when someone died. No one sat in circles to talk about what they missed. We went back to work. We kept things moving. We made jokes at the funeral and called it strength.

I didn't see grief as something sacred—I saw it as something you were supposed to hide.

Even now, when I feel it rise, my first instinct is to apologize for it. To explain it away. To move through it quickly so I don't make anyone uncomfortable. That response isn't mine alone. It belongs to generations of women before me who were taught to grieve in private, if at all.

Maybe you feel that too. The tightening in your chest when you need to cry. The shame that creeps in when you slow down. The fear that if you fall apart, you'll never come back together.

The truth is: falling apart was never the problem. Staying disconnected was.

- You are allowed to grieve without guilt.
- You are allowed to miss things that were never yours.
- You are allowed to speak to the younger version of yourself who waited far too long for someone to notice she was hurting.

Take your time here. Let this part of your healing move slowly. Grief is not asking for you to fix it. It's asking for you to stay present. To witness what was lost, without rushing to replace it.

If your voice trembles, let it. If your hands shake, let them. If your tears come at inconvenient times, let them fall anyway.

This is what reverence looks like.

You are not too much. You are not too late. You are right on time for your own return.

Shadow Sheet

The Sacred Space for Grief

This is your space. You don't have to make it pretty. You don't have to write complete sentences. You don't even have to make sense of it yet. Let these prompts meet you where you are. There is no "right way" to grieve — only your way. Give yourself permission to slow down. To listen. To tell the truth without editing it.

Take your time with these.

Reflection Prompts

1. What are you grieving right now — even if no one else would recognize it as grief?
   (Let this be a list, a letter, or a stream of thoughts. Nothing is too small to count.)

   ----

2. Who have you lost — emotionally, spiritually, and physically— that you never got the chance to fully mourn?
   (This may include people still living, people you never truly had, or parts of yourself you had to let go of.)

   ----

3. What grief were you taught to silence?
   (What messages did you receive — from family, culture, or society — about sadness, crying, or "being strong"?)

4. What do you wish someone had done for you while you were grieving?
   (What kind of care, presence, or ritual do you long for now?)

5. Write a love letter to the part of you that's still grieving.
   (Let it be soft. Let it be honest. Let it be yours.)

6. What grief in your body are you ready to acknowledge — even if you don't fully understand it yet?
   (Where do you feel it? What does it need from you?)

7. What would it look like to treat your grief with reverence instead of resistance?
   (What kind of ritual, movement, or expression would feel healing?)

This chapter may have stirred emotions that don't resolve right away. That's okay.

Grief isn't a problem to solve. It's a part of you that finally feels safe enough to be seen.

Close your eyes. Place your hand on your heart. Take a breath. You're doing it.

You're letting go. You're honoring what mattered. You're healing.

Chapter 10:

AWAKENING THE DIVINE FEMININE WITHIN

Reclaiming intuition, self-worth, boundaries, and embodied power

You weren't born doubting yourself. That came later.

You entered the world wide open—feeling everything, trusting your gut, reaching for connection. Somewhere along the way, the world taught you that softness was unsafe. That your emotions were too much. That your body wasn't yours. That your truth made people uncomfortable.

So you learned how to shrink. You learned how to be pleasing, palatable, and productive. This "shrinking" was a cultural trade-off. A century ago, psychiatrist Carl Jung observed that as we became a society obsessed with logic and power—what he called Logos—we began to sever our connection to our feeling and intuition, or Eros. Jung realized that this "feminine principle" wasn't just a religious idea, but a psychological necessity for wholeness. He spent his life's work proving that when we ignore this part of our psyche, we don't just lose our spirit; we lose ourselves.

You learned how to disconnect from the deeper voice inside you, the one that always knew what was right, even when no one else agreed.

That voice never left. She's still in there, waiting.

Some call her the Divine Feminine. While Jung gave us the language to understand her as a universal archetype—a blueprint for the soul—you don't have to be a scholar or a spiritualist to know her. She's not a goddess, a trend, or a performance. She's the part of you that knows when something's off before your mind can catch it. She's the part that cries at beauty. The part that says no without apology. The part that remembers who you were before life taught you to be afraid of your own power.

You may have lost touch with her, but she never stopped reaching for you.

This chapter is about re-entering that relationship. Not through perfection. Not through rules. Through remembering. Through breath. Through truth. Through trust.

She Was Always There

The Divine Feminine isn't something you become. She's something you remember.

She lives in the part of you that feels deeply, that knows without logic that breaks open in awe that speaks truth even when your voice shakes. She's not about being soft all the time. She's about being whole. She holds the rage, the tenderness, the boundaries, the intuition, the longing, and the power. She is not performing. She is present.

You've met her before though you may not have known what to call her. Maybe you felt her rise in the pit of your stomach when someone crossed your boundary. Maybe she whispered in your gut before you ever had words for why something felt wrong. Maybe you saw her in a moment of fierce clarity, a creative urge, a tear that refused to be swallowed.

She shows up when you stop apologizing for feeling. When you stop performing strength. When you stop negotiating your worth.

The world doesn't teach us to honor her. Most of us were raised to disconnect from her. We were taught to toughen up, to quiet our bodies, to fear our desire, to shrink our sensitivity. We learned to see intuition as irrational. Emotion as unstable. Power as dangerous.

It wasn't safe to let her lead, so we buried her. That doesn't mean she disappeared.

She was always there—waiting. Watching. Whispering beneath the noise.

When you began your shadow work, you weren't just digging up pain. You were making space. You were preparing the soil for something sacred to return. She rises through the cracks in your healing the places where your grief softened your armor and made room for something honest.

She doesn't ask for perfection. She asks for presence. For you to slow down long enough to hear her again.

Not everyone will understand this part of your journey. That's okay. This is between you and the truth inside your bones.

You're not just remembering her. You're remembering you.

The Buried Feminine – When Intuition Was Dangerous

You didn't let go of your intuition because you wanted to. You let go of it because, at some point, it felt safer to ignore it than to trust it. When we prioritize logic and production over feeling and connection, we don't just become more efficient; we become fragmented. You can see this "burying" in the quiet ways we negotiate away our power every day.

It's in the professional trade-off, like the woman who sits in a meeting and feels a "no" in her bones about a new project, yet ignores the pit in her stomach because she's afraid of being labeled "difficult." Six months later, she finds herself in the middle of a burnout that takes years to heal, all because her mind wouldn't let her listen to what her body knew on day one.

It's in the performance of our relationships, where we become "human clay," molding ourselves into whatever someone else needs us to be just to avoid conflict. We smile while our spirit is screaming, trading the messy, beautiful truth of how we feel for the safety of being easy to love. Eventually, our bodies start to speak in the only language we can't ignore: pain. What you may have labeled as chronic fatigue or a loss of spark is often just the Divine Feminine withdrawing. She doesn't fight for your attention; she simply goes quiet until you create a space safe enough for her to return

Reclaiming the Wild, the Worthy, and the Wise

She doesn't come back all at once.

She returns in pieces—in body chills and goosebumps, in gut feelings you finally trust, in the tears that rise up when you speak your truth without apologizing. She comes back in the quiet moments when you stop trying to be okay and just let yourself be real.

Reclaiming the Divine Feminine isn't about becoming someone new. It's about becoming someone honest. Someone whole. Someone you might've been all along, if the world hadn't taught you to be ashamed of her.

This energy isn't some feel-good trend or something only meant for people who have it all figured out. It's real. It's messy. It's about learning how to feel again—really feel.

It's about listening to yourself. Letting your body guide you, instead of tuning it out or pushing through like you've always had to.

The wild part of you, the instinctive one, she's not waiting for permission.

She's the part of you who knows when something doesn't feel right and walks away without apologizing. The one who dances barefoot in the kitchen just because it feels good, or screams into a pillow when she's reached her limit.

She's not here to be easy or pleasing. She's here to be free.

The worthy part of you is the one who doesn't need a reason to rest. The one who says no without guilt. The one who remembers that being lovable was never supposed to come with conditions. She doesn't need to earn her place. She is the place.

The wise part? That's the voice that's been whispering to you for years. The one that told you something was off. The one who asked for more. The one that nudged you toward healing before you even knew what that meant. She's not loud, but she's relentless. She doesn't forget.

You don't have to become all of this overnight. You don't need to force anything. You're not late. You're not behind. You're remembering. You're rebuilding trust with the parts of yourself you were told to bury. You're learning to let her take the lead again.

This isn't about being feminine in the way the world defines it. It's about being yours in the way only you can define.

You were never too wild. You were never too emotional. You were never too sensitive. You were never too much.

You were sacred. You still are.

Signs She's Waking Up

You might not notice her return right away. It doesn't always feel magical at first. Sometimes, it just feels uncomfortable—like your old life doesn't fit anymore, but you haven't figured out what does.

That's how she moves. Quiet. Unraveling. Alive.

You might find yourself feeling more sensitive than usual. Things you used to brush off now land differently. You cry when you didn't expect to. You say no sooner. You speak up even when your voice shakes. You walk away from situations you would've tolerated before. That's not weakness. That's wisdom waking up.

You might feel tired—deeply, soulfully tired. Not because something is wrong with you, but because you've spent so long carrying a version of yourself that was never fully yours. When the body starts to feel safe again, it lets go. It rests. It releases. That, too, is a sign.

I still think about that day—the one I described when my chest tightened so hard I thought something might be seriously wrong. That wasn't just a health scare. That was my body refusing to keep quiet. It came after years of ignoring what I felt, pushing through the pain, trying to hold everything together. That moment didn't feel spiritual at the time. It felt terrifying. Looking back, I see now that it was the beginning of something sacred. The Divine Feminine was never gone. She was waiting for a space where I could finally hear her again.

Maybe you're angry. That doesn't mean you're off track. It means your boundaries are returning. Rage is sacred when it comes from a place of truth. It burns off what no longer belongs.

You might feel more drawn to beauty. To music, color, texture, and movement. Your creativity starts to get excited beneath the surface again. Your senses sharpen. You catch your reflection and see someone different. Someone softer. Someone stronger.

Sometimes she returns through grief. Sometimes through joy. Sometimes, through the ache of realizing how much of yourself you abandoned just to be loved. That moment hurts—it also opens a door.

The Divine Feminine doesn't demand that you heal everything overnight. She asks you to notice. To stay present when your gut clenches, when your heart stirs, when your body whispers, enough.

You don't have to understand it all to know that something sacred is waking up.

That's her. That's you.

Practices to Call Her Back

The Divine Feminine doesn't need you to perform. She just needs space to breathe.

She responds to presence, not perfection. There's no single right way to remember her. What matters most is your willingness to slow down, to listen, and to soften into what's already inside you.

These aren't instructions. They're invitations.

1. Speak to yourself like someone sacred.

Your words are spells. Every time you call yourself lazy, crazy, too much, or not enough, your body takes note. Begin with this: "I hear you." When you feel something rise in your chest, don't dismiss it. Respond the way you wish someone would've responded to you when you were little—with warmth, with gentleness, with truth.

2. Follow what stirs, not what impresses.

Let desire lead, even if it doesn't make sense yet. The feminine within you is drawn to color, rhythm, texture, music, and beauty. She's not interested in productivity for the sake of validation. She wants connection. She wants creativity. She wants joy that doesn't need permission. Dance even when you're angry. Sing when you're tired. Wear what feels like you—even if it doesn't make sense to anyone else.

3. Let the body speak.

Intuition doesn't only live in the mind. It lives in the belly, in the chest, in the way your breath catches when something feels off. Create moments in your day to tune in. Place a hand on your heart. Ask, what do you need right now? Then wait. The answer may not come in words—it might come in a sigh, a tear, a stillness.

4. Honor what hurts.

You do not have to be unshakably calm to be powerful. Let the sadness move. Let the anger speak. Let the ache show you where you've been silencing yourself. There is nothing weak about needing to feel. You're not falling apart—you're letting what's been buried finally come home.

5. Choose softness without shame.

Softness isn't weakness. It's the willingness to be present, even when things are messy. When you choose rest over pushing through, connection over competition, truth over performing, you are calling her back. Softness doesn't mean collapse. It means remembering that your worth never depended on your hustle.

You don't need hours of silence or the perfect ritual to reconnect with her. You just need moments of truth. Moments where you stop pretending and come home to your body, your heart, your knowing.

She never left. She was waiting for you to return.

She's Always Been Yours

The Divine Feminine doesn't live in a title or a trend. She lives in the part of you that keeps rising, even after everything you've endured. She lives in the way you speak truth with shaking hands. In the way your body never gave up on you, even when you stopped listening. In the softness you're finally learning to allow.

You don't need to become anyone else to reclaim her. You just need to remember who you were before you learned to hide.

This chapter isn't asking you to master anything. It's offering you a mirror. Look into it without rushing. Let what you see be enough.

You already know her. You always have.

This time, you're choosing her on purpose.

Shadow Sheet

Awakening the Divine Feminine Within

These questions aren't here to fix you. They're here to bring you closer to the parts of you that have been silenced, softened, or shamed. Let this be a space to listen without judgment. Let her speak.

1. What did the world teach you about being soft, emotional, or intuitive?

   ----

2. Who first made you feel like those parts of you needed to be hidden or hardened?

   ----

3. When you look back, can you remember a moment your body spoke louder than your voice?

   ----

4. What was it trying to protect? What was it trying to tell you?

5. Where in your life have you abandoned your own knowing to be accepted, safe, or easy to love?

6. What did it cost you?

7. What feels wild in you now—the part that no longer wants to stay quiet or small?

8. What would it take to let her speak?

9. What does worthy feel like in your body—not as an idea, but as a sensation?

____
____
____
____

10. Can you name a moment, even a tiny one, when you felt it?

____
____
____
____

11. What does your intuition sound like?

____
____
____
____

12. How do you know when it's speaking—and how do you tend to ignore it?

____
____
____
____

13. Where are you still pushing, performing, or proving to be enough?

____
____
____
____

14. What version of you is asking to rest?

---

15. When you grieve the woman you had to be, what feelings come to the surface?

---

16. How do you honor that grief without rushing to fix it?

---

17. What does reclaiming the sacred feminine mean to you—not in theory, but in real life?

---

18. What would change if you embodied her just 10% more?

---

19. If the most sacred part of you were writing this page, what would she need you to see?

----

20. What truth is ready to be honored now?

Chapter 11:

THE REPARENTED SELF

Becoming the Mother You Never Had (But Always Needed)

There comes a moment in healing when the pain doesn't have to scream anymore. Not because it disappears, but because we finally learn how to sit with it. We stop abandoning ourselves in its presence. We lean in. We stay.

This is the part of the journey where we stop waiting for someone else to show up and do the hard parts for us. We begin showing up for ourselves. We begin building safety where there used to be fear, gentleness where there used to be silence, and structure where there used to be chaos.

Reparenting doesn't mean erasing your past or pretending your needs were never neglected. It means creating something new, something steadier, something that finally knows how to hold the version of you that was always left holding everything alone.

It means saying things to yourself that no one ever said to you when you needed it most:

"You don't have to keep trying so hard."

"You're safe now."

"You still matter when you're not doing anything for anyone."

"You're not broken because you feel things deeply."

This isn't about perfection. This is about presence.

Learning how to mother yourself with compassion, care, and consistency changes everything.

It doesn't happen all at once, but it begins here.

What Reparenting Really Means

The word "reparenting" gets used a lot in healing spaces, but many people don't actually understand what it means or why it matters.

To reparent yourself means to create the kind of internal environment you didn't grow up with. It means listening to yourself when the old voices in your head would rather shut you down. It means choosing to care for your needs even when the world taught you to ignore them.

Most of us were raised to believe that emotions were inconvenient or dramatic. We were told to toughen up, get over it, or smile through the pain. Many of us were punished for crying or labeled "too sensitive" for speaking our truth. That kind of early conditioning teaches you to turn away from yourself.

Reparenting turns you back toward your truth, gently and consistently.

This isn't about blaming your parents or staying stuck in the past. It's about becoming aware of the ways your inner world was shaped, and choosing to take responsibility for what happens now. You don't have to keep living in patterns that began in pain. You are allowed to build new ones that begin in love.

Reparenting looks like:

- Pausing when you feel overwhelmed, instead of pushing harder.
- Saying no, even if it disappoints someone.
- Choosing rest without guilt.
- Reminding yourself that you are worthy of kindness, even when you mess up.

It also means having your own back. Not just in the big moments, but in the small ones — the late nights, the hard mornings, the shaky boundaries you're still learning how to hold. You become the steady hand, the calm voice, the presence that never leaves.

Most of us didn't get that growing up.

We got rules, expectations, and survival strategies.

We learned how to perform. We learned how to pretend.

But we didn't learn how to love ourselves through the mess.

Reparenting teaches us how to do that.

It gives us permission to be human, while also holding ourselves accountable to the kind of life we truly want.

This is not about being perfect at healing. It's about practicing care in moments where you used to disappear. That is the foundation. That is the shift.

The Voice of the Inner Mother

The inner mother isn't just an idea. She is a voice, a presence, a pattern you begin to choose. For many of us, she didn't exist when we were young. We were raised by women who were overwhelmed, unavailable, or emotionally distant. We learned how to survive without being held.

That survival made us strong, but it also left us with a deep ache — a longing for softness, steadiness, and someone who knew how to stay.

The voice of the inner mother begins quietly. Sometimes it shows up as a whisper that says, "It's okay to rest," or "You didn't deserve that." Other times, it comes through as a feeling — a slow breath, a softened jaw, a decision not to punish yourself for being human.

This voice doesn't come naturally at first. Most of us were trained to speak to ourselves like drill sergeants or judges. We learned that love had to be earned, comfort had to be postponed, and boundaries made us selfish. That internal noise takes time to unlearn.

For a long time, I didn't know how to be kind to myself unless I thought I had earned it. If I wasn't being productive, I didn't feel like I mattered. If I made a mistake, I would spiral into shame.

I didn't realize how unkind I was being until I started paying attention to the way I spoke to myself. I began asking simple questions like, "Who said that?" or "Where have I heard this before?" Most of the time, the voice in my head wasn't mine. It came from past criticism—things I had heard from others and unknowingly turned into my own self-talk.

Becoming aware of that was the beginning.

Reparenting yourself isn't about pretending to love every part of you. It's not about forcing some perfect version of self-acceptance. It's about noticing the small, painful moments when your inner child flinches—and choosing to stay with her.

It's about using the same gentleness you'd offer a child who is scared, overwhelmed, or simply tired from trying so hard.

The voice of the inner mother is steady. She doesn't rush your healing. She doesn't demand perfection. She doesn't call you weak when you need to fall apart.

You can learn to become her.

That voice might not feel natural yet. You may have to practice it, again and again, until it becomes familiar. Until it becomes yours.

Boundaries as Protection, Not Punishment

Many of us were taught that boundaries hurt people. That saying no would make us difficult or selfish. We learned to read the room instead of our own body. We learned to silence our discomfort to keep the peace. The more we over-functioned, the more praise we received. The more we tolerated, the more we were trusted.

We internalized the belief that connection required self-abandonment, that belief lives in the nervous system. It's not just emotional — it's physiological. When you've grown up in unpredictable or emotionally unsafe environments, your body learns to treat self-protection as a threat.

This is where the trauma response known as fawning often develops. It's not about being nice — it's about being hyper-aware of others' needs and moods in order to avoid conflict, rejection, or emotional withdrawal. It's about staying safe through compliance. Fawning is especially common in those who experienced childhood emotional neglect, inconsistent parenting, or enmeshment.

Boundaries disrupt that survival pattern. They remind the body that you are no longer stuck in the past — that you are no longer a child navigating unsafe dynamics without support.

Boundaries help you remember that your voice matters, your needs matter, and your choices are your own.

A boundary is not a punishment. It's not something you use to hurt or control someone.

A boundary is a clear line that says, "This is where I stop leaving myself behind."

Boundaries can be both external and internal. External boundaries might look like saying no to plans that leave you drained, not answering calls from people who only take, or telling someone how you expect to be treated.

Internal boundaries are the ones you set with yourself. They might sound like, "I will not keep pushing through exhaustion." Or, "I won't speak to myself with cruelty." Or, "I won't stay in situations that hurt me, just because they feel familiar."

For many people who've experienced trauma, setting a boundary can bring up guilt. That doesn't mean you're doing something wrong. It means your nervous system is adjusting to a new way of being.

You're learning that real care goes both ways. You're teaching yourself that safety doesn't have to mean silence. And that you don't have to trade your truth for love.

From a clinical lens, boundary work supports post-traumatic growth and attachment repair. It builds interoception — the ability to notice what you're feeling inside your body. It helps restore a sense of personal agency, which is often lost in early trauma. Agency means remembering you have the right to choose your own needs, your own truth, and your own life—even when someone once made you feel like you didn't.

You don't have to make boundaries complicated.

You don't need to over-explain.

You don't need to convince anyone.

You get to say:

- "This doesn't feel good for me."
- "I need space."
- "That doesn't work for me anymore."
- "I'm not available for this."

Those sentences might shake your voice the first time. Your heart might race. Your hands might tremble. That doesn't mean you're doing it wrong. That means you're healing.

You may lose some connections that were built on your silence. That's part of the grief.

You will also gain a version of yourself that no longer sacrifices peace for proximity.

That is the gift.

Boundaries are not about control. They are about clarity.

They don't push people away. They show you who is willing to walk beside you without asking you to betray yourself in the process.

This is what protection looks like when it's rooted in self-respect instead of fear.

Rituals of Daily Care

Healing doesn't happen in one big moment of clarity. It happens in the small things — the quiet rituals, the choices no one else sees, the moments when you decide not to abandon yourself again.

Daily care is how reparenting becomes real.

It's how the inner mother stops being a concept and becomes a presence.

It's how you remind your body and nervous system, over and over, that you are no longer unsafe.

Many trauma survivors struggle with consistency.

This isn't laziness or lack of willpower — it's often the result of a nervous system stuck in survival mode. If you spent your childhood in chaos, neglect, or emotional unpredictability, routines might feel unfamiliar or even threatening. Structure may have been used as a weapon instead of a support. You may have learned to stay hyper-vigilant, ready to adapt, always waiting for the next shift.

Ritual is different from rigidity.

Rituals are chosen. They are gentle. They are meaningful. They speak to the soul and the body at the same time.

Rituals of daily care can include:

- Waking slowly and placing your hand on your heart before reaching for your phone
- Drinking water mindfully, reminding your body it deserves nourishment
- Stretching or moving in a way that releases tension instead of punishing it
- Checking in with your feelings instead of overriding them
- Using affirming language, especially during difficult moments ("I can be with myself in this")

- Creating evening rhythms that signal safety and softness — turning down lights, lighting a candle, speaking kindly to your body before sleep

These practices might seem small, but their impact runs deep. They begin to rebuild what early trauma often takes away — your sense of rhythm, safety, and connection to yourself.

From a nervous system perspective, these rituals help bring your body out of survival mode. They calm the fight-or-flight response and support a more grounded, connected state.

They also help your brain form new patterns. Each time you choose care, each time you return to your body with kindness, you're strengthening the parts of you that know how to feel, how to rest, how to choose, and how to connect without fear.

You don't need a perfect morning routine or a strict schedule.

You just need a few consistent, intentional moments where you choose yourself.

You begin to parent the younger parts of you who were rushed, dismissed, or overlooked.

I've learned that some of my most powerful healing has come through very ordinary moments: brushing my hair with patience, lighting incense before journaling, speaking out loud to my inner child and saying, "I've got you now."

This is how the reparented self is built.

Not through performance, but through presence.

Not through perfection, but through repetition.

Each small act of care becomes a brick in the foundation of a life that feels safe to live in.

That safety begins inside you — and it begins today.

Building Trust With Yourself

Rebuilding trust with yourself is tender, honest work. It's not always easy, but it changes everything.

For people who have lived through trauma, trust doesn't start with confidence. It starts with a willingness. A willingness to stay. To try. To listen, even when it feels unfamiliar. Especially if you've spent years ignoring your own needs just to get through.

When you've been gaslit, neglected, or dismissed over and over, the first person you stop trusting is yourself. You begin to question your feelings. You second-guess your instincts. You start looking to others for answers, because at some point, someone taught you that your inner voice didn't matter.

In trauma recovery, this is sometimes called *self-betrayal conditioning*. It often begins in childhood. Maybe a parent told you, you weren't cold when you were clearly shivering. Or said you were "too sensitive" when you were hurt. I remember being told, "That's not your favorite color," like I couldn't even be trusted to know my own preferences.

Over time, your body starts to believe that your truth isn't reliable. That it's not safe to trust what you feel. So you learn to rely on others for what's real. You tune in to everyone else's needs and slowly lose touch with your own.

Reparenting helps break that cycle. It gives you small, daily chances to practice showing up for yourself with kindness and consistency. It doesn't have to be perfect. It just needs to be real. That's how you start becoming your own steady place to land.

✦ *Self-Trust Is Built, Not Inherited*

Many people assume that self-trust is either something you have or don't have. In reality, it's a relational skill — one that can be learned, strengthened, and repaired over time.

Here's the hard truth: you can't build trust with yourself by thinking about it. You build it by behaving differently. You build it by keeping promises to yourself — especially the ones no one else knows about. You build it by showing up for your inner child even when it feels inconvenient or uncomfortable.

This isn't about proving anything. It's about consistency, kindness, and follow-through.

✦ *How We Betray Ourselves (Often Without Realizing)*

Self-betrayal isn't always loud. It often sounds like:

- Agreeing to something while your chest tightens and your gut says no
- Smiling through pain to make someone else comfortable
- Justifying or explaining away mistreatment
- Making yourself small so others don't feel insecure
- Apologizing for needs that are basic and human
- Abandoning rest, joy, or boundaries to avoid guilt

Each of these moments may seem small on the surface but to your nervous system, they're evidence that your truth doesn't matter. Over time, these micro-moments add up to a deep inner belief: *"I can't trust myself to protect me."*

The antidote is not to get it perfect. The antidote is to begin again, with compassion.

✦ *How We Repair Trust With Ourselves*

Self-trust is rebuilt in small, embodied steps. Here's what that can look like:

1. Make and keep micro-promises.

Say, "I'll go to bed at 10 tonight," and follow through. Say, "I'll leave the room when I feel overstimulated," and actually do it. These promises might feel small, but they communicate safety to your inner world. They say, "You matter enough for me to listen."

2. Build an internal feedback loop.

After making a choice, pause and ask:

- Did that feel aligned?
- Did I honor my body's signals?
- Do I feel resentment or relief?

This kind of reflection builds your internal compass. It strengthens your capacity for interoception, the clinical term for perceiving internal sensations and signals

3. Speak the truth, even if it's messy.

You don't need to be eloquent or perfectly regulated to be honest. You just need to practice naming what's real. "This feels heavy." "I'm not okay with this." "I need a break." Truth is a muscle — and like any muscle, it gets stronger the more you use it.

4. Repair after rupture.

You will miss things. You will betray yourself again. That's not failure. That's part of the process. What matters most is that you notice, pause, and return. That moment of repair — saying, "That wasn't what I wanted for myself, and I will do better" — is what builds trust. Not perfection. Repair.

5. Create consistent check-ins.

Every morning or evening, ask yourself:

- What do I need emotionally?
- What am I avoiding?
- What does my body want today?
- Where do I need to say no?

These questions teach your nervous system that you are safe to connect with. They create an internal rhythm — something trauma often interrupts.

✦ Self-Trust Feels Different in the Body

Trust is not just a mindset. It's a felt sense. When you trust yourself, your body relaxes. Your decisions feel quieter. Your boundaries feel less threatening. You start to feel at home in your own skin, even when life is hard.

From a clinical perspective, this is a sign of nervous system regulation. Your vagus nerve begins to activate your parasympathetic state — allowing you to feel calm, connected, and clear. This is not just emotional. It's physical.

You begin to embody safety.

You stop reacting to old scripts.

You start responding from inner alignment.

This is what real empowerment looks like — not a performative strength, but a rooted, steady trust that says, "I am with myself now."

✦ Reparenting Is a Trust-Building Practice

You don't have to love yourself completely to begin trusting yourself. You just need to stay with yourself.

Each time you listen to your gut, speak your truth, or soothe your nervous system instead of shaming it, you build trust. Each time you pause instead of push, or rest instead of hustle, or protect your energy instead of overextend — you send the message, "I will not abandon you again."

That is the reparented self.

Not just healed — but trustworthy.

Not just aware — but integrated.

Not just surviving — but choosing.

This is how you learn to be the one who never leaves.

Reparenting the Inner Child in Real Time

Reparenting is not something you master. It is something you return to again and again, especially when life feels messy.

It is easy to be kind to yourself when everything is calm. The real challenge is staying kind when shame creeps in, when your boundaries are crossed, or when you start crying over something that seems too small to matter.

That is when the work truly begins.

Your inner child is not just a memory. She lives in your body. She shows up when you feel rejected, ignored, or unseen. She pulls back when someone raises their voice. She freezes when you feel overwhelmed. She panics when love feels distant or uncertain.

Most of the time, she does not use words. She speaks through your body. You might feel a racing heart. A heavy pit in your stomach. An ache that you cannot explain.

In these moments, it is easy to blame yourself. It feels safer to shut down than to feel what is really happening. You might try to push through instead of saying what you need.

But reparenting asks something different. It asks you to stay.

This work begins with noticing when the child in you is present. Then, it asks you to respond with care instead of control. With gentleness instead of silence. With presence instead of pressure.

✦ *Recognizing When the Inner Child Is Being Triggered*

Reparenting in real time starts with awareness. Your inner child doesn't always speak in words — she shows up through your emotions, reactions, and fears. If she's been triggered, you may notice:

- A sudden feeling of abandonment or rejection
- Emotional reactions that seem bigger than the situation
- Shame, fear, or the urge to hide
- People-pleasing or over-explaining
- Physical signals like tightness in the chest, shallow breath, or dissociation

These are not signs of weakness. They are messages from the parts of you that still need to feel safe.

There is no need to analyze the feeling away. What helps is attending to it with gentleness.

✦ *Responding with Comfort Instead of Criticism*

The voice of the inner mother becomes essential here. In the middle of a trigger or regression, speak to yourself the way you would speak to a child who's overwhelmed.

Instead of asking "What's wrong with me?" try saying:

- "I see you. This hurts, and I'm here."
- "This makes sense. It reminds you of before."
- "You're not alone this time."

- "You're allowed to feel this."

The words matter. So does the tone. Calm, steady presence will do more for your nervous system than logic ever could. Even if your adult self feels unsteady, the act of choosing compassion is the medicine.

✦ *Releasing the Grief That Was Never Witnessed*

Many people were never given the chance to grieve what they lost. Not just loved ones, but the care that never came. The safety that was never there. The kind of childhood that had to be survived instead of enjoyed.

That kind of grief does not go away on its own. It stays in the body until it has a chance to move.

Reparenting creates space for that grief to be felt. You are allowed to miss the things you never received. It is okay to grieve the mother who couldn't be there for you. There is no shame in hurting over something no one ever acknowledged.

This grief is not too much. It is not a burden. It matters. It deserves time, care, and space to be honored.

✦ *Practicing Forgiveness for the Times You Didn't Know How*

You won't get this right every time.

There will be moments when you shut down again. You might miss the signs. You might slip back into old habits that no longer feel good.

That doesn't mean you've failed.

These moments are part of healing. They make the process real. Not perfect, but honest.

The part of you that is learning to heal isn't asking for perfection. She is asking you to come back.

When you forget her, return. When you mess up, repair the connection. These small acts build more trust than any version of getting it all right ever could.

Try saying:

- "I didn't know better, and now I'm learning."
- "I forgive myself for the ways I coped."
- "My needs are not a burden."
- "Even when I forget, I still deserve care."

These aren't just phrases. They're offerings — small altars of truth you return to, again and again.

✦ *The Body Remembers — and You Can Respond Differently Now*

Your body remembers what you've been through. It holds every moment you didn't feel safe. But it can also remember what it's like to feel loved, cared for, and comforted.

When something pulls you back into the past, your nervous system needs more than just understanding. It needs evidence that things are different now.

Let your breath slow down. Put a hand on your heart. Feel your feet on the ground. These aren't small things. They are the beginning of safety.

This is what it means to ground yourself.

It's the practice of coming back to the present. Back to your breath, your body, and what's real right now. Grounding isn't about pretending everything is okay. It's about helping your nervous system feel that you are no longer stuck in what once was.

It's how you remind yourself: I'm here. I'm safe. I'm in this moment now.

Reparenting isn't about getting it all right. It's about being the one who stays, especially when things feel hard. It's about choosing to stay present, again and again, until it becomes something you can trust.

You are not too late to become the protector you always needed.

You are not unworthy because you missed it before.

You are not too broken to learn how to listen to yourself with love.

Healing begins here. It begins now. And it begins again, every time you return to the child in you and say, "I've got you. I always will."

Becoming Someone You Can Count On

Reparenting is not a destination you reach. It's a devotion. A promise to yourself that says,

"I will not keep abandoning me."

You may not have had the mother you needed.

You may have grown up learning to hide your needs, to silence your truth, to work twice as hard for half as much love.

You may have carried the weight of unmet grief, and the ache of being the strong one for far too long.

That story does not end here.

This is the moment when the child in you finally feels someone show up. Not to rescue her. Not to fix her. But to love her exactly as she is.

To see her pain without turning away. To make space for her fear. To offer steadiness, kindness, and safety — again and again — until it no longer feels strange to receive it.

You are not too late to become someone trustworthy.

You are not too far gone to rebuild self-respect.

You are not unworthy just because no one showed you how to believe in yourself before now.

You are allowed to be new here.

Reparenting doesn't mean you always feel confident. It means you are willing to stay — even when the shame comes, even when the fear rises, even when old patterns try to pull you back.

You get to pause.

You get to soften.

You get to speak gently to the parts of you who once had no one.

That's what changes everything. Not perfection. Not performance.

Just presence — sacred, daily, imperfect presence.

When you become the one who stays, the one who listens, the one who nurtures and protects, you stop chasing love that costs you your peace.

You stop proving yourself to people who don't know how to see you.

You stop outsourcing your worth to circumstances you can't control.

Instead, you come home — not to the place you were raised, but to the self you are raising now.

The reparented self is not a fixed version of you.

She is a living, breathing truth:

You can be both the one who was hurt and the one who heals.

You can be the mother you never had — the daughter who finally feels safe to rest.

Humans can learn.

Healing is always allowed to begin again.

Shadow Sheet

The Reparented Self

Becoming the Mother You Never Had (But Always Needed)

1. What did you most need to hear as a child that you never received?

   ----

2. Where in your life today do you still find yourself unconsciously waiting for someone else to say it?

   ----

3. When do you tend to emotionally abandon yourself?

   ----

4. What does that moment cost you — in peace, presence, or self-trust?

   ----

5. What tone does your inner critic take when you're struggling?

6. If a child you loved were spoken to in that tone, how would you intervene?

7. What were you taught about rest, softness, or emotional needs?

8. How have those teachings shaped your relationship with your own vulnerability?

9. What boundary have you been afraid to set because of guilt or fear of rejection?

10. What would protecting your peace in that situation say to your inner child?

11. What is one simple daily act of care your inner child would recognize as love?

12. What resistance comes up when you imagine doing it consistently?

13. Where have you been hard on yourself just for surviving?

14. Can you meet that version of you with compassion instead of critique?

----

15. What are your body's signals when your inner child is triggered or overwhelmed?

----

16. How can you respond in those moments like someone who knows how to stay?

----

17. What promise can you make to yourself now that your younger self never got to hear?

----

18. How will you prove to her that this time, you mean it?

----

19. If you could become the mother you always needed, how would you begin treating yourself today?

----

20. What would need to shift — in how you speak, soothe, protect, or prioritize yourself?

Chapter 12:

THE EMBODIED SELF

Learning to Feel Safe in Your Own Body Again

Some parts of healing feel like waking up. But Shadow Work feels more like returning to a house you once had to set on fire just to stay warm in the middle of a blizzard. You didn't leave because you were 'broken'; you left because the smoke became too thick to breathe. Now, the fire has died down, and you are stepping back into the ruins to see what survived.

This chapter is about that return.

Your body is the vault for the parts of you that were too loud, too angry, or too 'much' for the world to handle. It didn't just 'bury' your mind's secrets; it mummified them in your fascia and tucked them behind your ribcage. Every unexplained ache is a Shadow trying to tell you its name.

For many of us, the body didn't feel like a safe place to be. So we left it in the ways we knew how.

We didn't just 'move away' from our bodies. We evicted ourselves. We became ghosts haunting our own lives, floating a few inches above the floor because landing felt like a collision. This wasn't a lack of willpower; it was a tactical retreat.

But now, we get to return.

Stillness didn't always feel peaceful. Presence didn't always feel safe. Even joy felt suspicious at times. The body carried too much. It felt unfamiliar, unpredictable, heavy. Many of us learned to live outside of it, observing from a distance, numbing what we couldn't process.

Returning to the body doesn't happen all at once. It begins with permission. Permission to slow down. Permission to listen. Permission to be gentle with the places that still flinch, tremble, or tighten at the thought of being truly seen.

You were never meant to live at war with yourself. The body was never the enemy. It adapted to help you survive what you didn't yet have words for. Every dissociation, every shutdown, every ache was a form of protection. Now that you are no longer in danger, the invitation is changing.

This part of the healing asks you to come home, not to the body you were taught to control, but to the one you are learning to love. Not to the body that was shaped by trauma, but to the one that is still soft enough to feel, brave enough to stay, and wise enough to heal.

You are allowed to reclaim it.

You are allowed to listen again.

You are allowed to live fully here, not just in thought, but in breath, in movement, in rhythm, in truth. There is no rush.

There is no perfect way. Only a steady return to the place inside you that was never meant to be abandoned.

This is where embodiment begins.

The Disconnected Body

There was a time I didn't even know I had left my body. I was going through the motions. I was doing what needed to be done. I was performing the role of someone who was okay.

But deep down, something had gone quiet. Something in me had pulled away.

Disconnection doesn't always come in loud or dramatic ways. Sometimes it shows up like a quiet fog. You don't feel much of anything—not sadness, not joy. Just numbness.

You keep moving. You keep working. You keep smiling. On the outside, everything seems fine. But inside, you feel far from yourself.

For many trauma survivors, this is how it begins — not with a single moment of collapse, but with a slow, subtle separation from the body. A soft detachment that forms over time when the body doesn't feel like a safe place to be.

That disconnection is not a flaw.

It is a survival response.

When you're young and overwhelmed, when the fear is too big or the grief too much, your nervous system does what it must. It protects you by pulling you away from the source of pain. When fight or flight isn't an option, the body chooses freeze.

This isn't a weakness. This is intelligence.

The nervous system has a built-in sequence of survival responses: fight, flight, freeze, and fawn. Fight means stand your ground. Flight means running. Fawn means appease. Freeze is the last line of defense.

Your body is always trying to protect you. It scans for danger and decides whether you have the strength, the power, or the support to respond.

If it senses that fighting back will only make things worse—or that running isn't an option—it turns inward instead.

This is where the freeze response begins.

Freeze happens when there's no safe way out and no safe way through. It's the response of someone who feels overwhelmed and trapped.

It's what happens to the child who can't leave the room. Or the person who knows that speaking up will only lead to more harm.

When every other option feels dangerous, freeze becomes the only way to survive.

To freeze is to go still and quiet, hoping not to be noticed. It's the instinct to disappear. To become unreachable.

In that moment, your body starts to shut down. Sensations go numb. Your heart rate slows. Your awareness pulls away.

You don't choose it. It happens automatically.

This is your nervous system stepping in to protect you — not just your body, but your mind. It's doing what it knows to do to help you survive when things feel too overwhelming to handle.

Freeze may not look heroic, but it's what saved you. It kept you from feeling the full impact of what you weren't ready to hold.

Freeze gave you a way to survive something that should have never happened.

For those of us who grew up in places where fighting back or running away wasn't possible—because of our age, fear, trauma, or dependence—freezing became the safest option. It was how we stayed alive.

Even now, long after the danger has passed, your body might still hold on to that response. Not because something is wrong with you, but because disappearing once kept you safe.

You learned to leave before you could be hurt. You learned to float above your feelings. You trained yourself to stay quiet, small, and invisible.

After a while, it started to feel normal. You didn't even realize you were numb. You just felt tired all the time. Or restless. Or like you didn't quite belong in your own body.

Some people mistake this for strength. They say, "You're so calm under pressure," or "Nothing rattles you." The truth is, you're not calm. You're shut down. You're holding everything inside because letting it out feels dangerous.

That version of you was brave. She survived the storm by becoming invisible to it.

Still, there comes a point in healing where disconnection starts to feel less like safety and more like silence. You begin to miss the parts of yourself that went quiet. You begin to long for your voice, your breath, your sense of aliveness.

The return to your body won't feel natural at first.

It might feel like grief.

It might feel like panic.

It might feel like you're waking up in a place you don't recognize.

This is not a step backward. It's a step toward wholeness. The body is not punishing you when it trembles. It is remembering that it no longer needs to carry everything alone.

Coming back begins with noticing. A deep breath. A clenched jaw. A racing heart. A heavy stillness in the chest. These are not signs of failure. These are signals. Invitations. Each one asking, "Can you stay with me this time?"

You don't need to feel everything all at once. You don't have to force yourself into presence. You just need to begin noticing that you're still here. This body — your body — has been waiting for you. Not with shame. Not with judgment.

With patience. With memory. With truth. You have not missed your chance to return.

Safety Before Sensation

Coming back to your body sounds like a beautiful idea—until you actually try it.

The books, the meditations, the wellness posts make it seem peaceful. For those of us who lived disconnected for years, presence doesn't always feel like safety. At first, it might feel like panic. Sometimes it feels like grief. Sometimes it feels like a trap.

The nervous system doesn't care about your good intentions. It doesn't care how many breathwork techniques you know. It cares about safety—real safety, the kind your body can feel, not just understand.

If the body still believes it's in danger, even something as gentle as a body scan can trigger a stress response. You might feel tension instead of calm. You might dissociate. You might burst into tears for reasons you can't explain. All of this is normal. None of this means you're doing it wrong. Your body is not resisting healing—it's protecting you the only way it knows how.

When trauma taught you to leave your body to survive, the return has to happen slowly. It cannot be forced. Safety must come before sensation. That's the rule the nervous system follows.

So we begin not by diving into emotion or trying to feel everything at once. We begin with regulation. With a presence that doesn't overwhelm. With cues that tell the body, You are safe now. You don't have to brace anymore.

That starts with the most basic rhythms. Feel your feet on the floor. Notice the support of the chair beneath you. Let your eyes settle on something steady in the room. Breathe—not deeply, not forcefully. Just gently. Just enough. Touch your own chest or belly with warmth. Whisper to yourself, I'm right here.

These aren't performance tools. They're trust-building signals. They tell your nervous system, We're not rushing. We're not leaving. We're not forcing. They say, You don't have to shut down. You don't have to disappear. I will stay with you.

Sometimes you need another person to help you get there. A therapist. A partner. A healer who can hold steady while you slowly re-enter your own body. This is called co-regulation—letting someone else's calm anchor your own. It's one of the most natural ways to restore nervous system safety, yet so many of us were never taught how to receive it.

You don't have to prove your capacity for solitude. You don't have to heal in isolation. Receiving safety is just as important as generating it. This part of the journey will ask you to slow down, even when your mind wants to rush.

It will ask you to pause, even when the urgency returns. It will ask you to listen gently, especially when old patterns shout for you to shut it all out.

Reconnection is not about pushing yourself into presence. It's about making a presence a place that feels safe to return to.

Learning the Language of the Body

The body doesn't use words. It speaks through signals.

Tight shoulders. A heavy feeling in your stomach. A lump in your throat. A heart that won't slow down.

These aren't random or annoying symptoms. They're messages. Gentle cues from your nervous system, asking for your attention.

But when you've spent years learning to ignore or override your body's truth, those signals can start to feel like a problem—or even like the enemy.

For years, you may have told yourself to calm down, toughen up, stop crying, and get over it. You might have silenced your pain to be accepted. You might have ignored your needs to avoid conflict. You might have swallowed every "no" because you were taught that your instincts couldn't be trusted.

Eventually, your body stops speaking clearly. Not because it has nothing to say, but because it doesn't believe anyone is listening.

Part of coming back to your body is learning how to listen again.

It means relearning the language of sensation, emotion, and instinct. It means noticing the difference between fear and exhaustion. Between the kind of tension that says, "I don't feel safe," and the kind that says, "I'm carrying too much."

This kind of awareness takes time. It won't happen all at once.

You might start by simply paying attention to what you feel, without trying to fix it. You might pause during the day and ask yourself, "What's going on in my chest? In my jaw? In my hands?"

You might begin keeping a body journal, writing down what you notice—how your body feels, how your emotions shift.

This is how you start rebuilding the connection. Slowly, gently, one moment at a time.

As the awareness grows, so does trust.

You begin to understand that the tightness isn't random—it's a boundary you didn't speak. The racing heart isn't overreacting—it's reacting to something your mind tried to minimize. The tears that come out of nowhere aren't weakness—they're grief that finally feels safe enough to surface.

The body remembers what the mind forgets, and in learning to listen, you begin to reclaim parts of yourself you didn't know you'd lost. Parts that stopped speaking because no one answered. Parts that protected you by going quiet. Parts that carried everything so you could function.

Embodiment is not about being perfectly present every moment. It's about having the courage to turn toward yourself instead of away. It's about letting your body be more than a burden to manage or a tool to perform with. It's about letting it become a place of truth, intuition, and healing.

This is how you begin to speak your own language again. One signal at a time. One breath at a time. One soft return after another.

When the Body Becomes the Battleground

When safety isn't available through connection, the body becomes the battlefield. It carries what couldn't be expressed. It absorbs what others refused to hold. It reflects what was never spoken aloud.

For some, that looks like tension locked into every muscle. For others, it becomes a chronic illness, fatigue, or a pain that doctors can't explain. The body remembers not just the moments of impact, but the years of silence that followed. It holds the shame, the fear, and the powerlessness. It holds the bracing.

You may not have had the language for trauma when it happened, but your body did. It tightened, it protected, it froze, it numbed. Those patterns didn't disappear just because the danger ended. They lingered, looping underneath the surface, until the body became a site of struggle instead of peace.

This is how the war turns inward.

You might feel frustrated when your body doesn't relax during meditation. You might shame yourself for emotional eating, for holding tension, or for needing more rest than usual. You might even get angry when your body doesn't heal the way you thought it should—or the way others expect it to.

It can turn into a painful cycle.

Your body is trying to protect you, but you end up blaming it for how it responds. You feel tired, disconnected, and overwhelmed—and then judge yourself for not bouncing back quickly.

But none of this is your fault. These are the quiet aftershocks of surviving what your body was never meant to carry alone.

Healing begins by stepping out of the war.

That means refusing to shame your symptoms. It means honoring your fatigue instead of resenting it. It means listening to your body's resistance with curiosity instead of control. Every time you choose compassion over criticism, your nervous system gets a new message: You are not the problem. You are not being punished. You are safe enough to soften.

This doesn't mean bypassing the pain. It means creating the conditions where your body can let go of the fight. Not because it was forced to, but because it finally believes it's allowed to.

You don't have to be at war with yourself to be whole. You are not broken. You are responding to the life you lived. Now, you are choosing something different

Embodiment After Trauma — What It Actually Looks Like

Embodiment is often painted as peaceful- but the truth is, when you first return to your body after trauma, it doesn't always feel like coming home. Sometimes it feels like stepping into a house that's been boarded up for years—where grief clings to the walls and every door creaks with memories you tried to forget.

You might expect to feel calm once you start breathing again. Instead, your chest tightens. Your skin feels too sensitive. Emotions rise without context—rage, longing, sorrow—and it's easy to wonder if something is wrong with you.

Nothing is wrong. This is an embodiment after trauma. It's messy. It's unpredictable. It's loud in places you were taught to be quiet. You might find yourself crying in the grocery store because the sound of glass shattering reminds your body of a night you never talk about. You might suddenly need to be alone for days, not because you're isolating, but because your nervous system is finally allowed to rest. You might feel cravings for movement, for rhythm, for touch—not because you're broken, but because your body is remembering what it means to be alive.

Healing doesn't happen in a straight line. Some days, embodiment feels like warm tea and soft blankets. Other days, it feels like shaking, sweating, screaming into a pillow. Your body doesn't follow your calendar. It doesn't care if you "have time for this." When it begins to thaw, it releases what's been frozen, and what surfaces is everything you thought you'd buried well enough to forget.

You might feel exhausted. You might feel confused. You might even feel guilty for the parts of you that are still scared to feel. That doesn't mean you're doing it wrong. Embodiment is not a performance. It's not a checklist. It's not a polished morning routine on Instagram.

It's the way your body whispers, "I'm still here," after decades of being ignored. It's letting your stomach unclench without needing to justify it. It's noticeable that your shoulders are no longer pulled to your ears. It's realizing that softness can live alongside survival.

You don't have to love every part of your body to live inside it. You just have to let it be honest. Let it be messy. Let it belong to you again.

When the Body Feels Unsafe

Not every survivor feels safe returning to their body.

For many people, the body holds memories that are still alive beneath the surface. Sometimes, pain is the only feeling that feels familiar.

Coming back into the body doesn't always feel like healing. At first, it can feel like being thrown back into the fire.

When your body holds stories of violation, rejection, or abandonment, being present with it can feel overwhelming—even unbearable.

This part of the healing process is rarely talked about. We're often told to take deep breaths, regulate our emotions, and listen to our body's wisdom. But few people say how terrifying it can be to actually feel what the body has been carrying.

For some, the body doesn't feel like home. It feels like a haunted house.

Growing up without consistent safety distorts our relationship with the body. Needs were either ignored, punished, or unmet. Over time, the body began to flinch from contact, even when no harm was intended. It longed to be held while simultaneously recoiling from touch. This creates a pattern of contradiction—too much sensation, not enough grounding—where the nervous system doesn't know what to trust.

This is when survival strategies can turn inward.

When I was around eight years old, I began hurting myself. At the time, I didn't have words for what I was feeling. I only knew that something hurt deeply inside me, and physical pain gave that hurt somewhere to land.

I was careful about it. I used scratches from animals or from playing outside as an excuse. Coming home with marks wasn't unusual for me, so no one questioned it at first.

When people started to notice, I forced myself to stop. Not because the pain had gone away, but because the fear of being seen and shamed felt worse than the pain itself.

A few years later, I began reaching for other coping mechanisms. Smoking and drinking became my new outlets. They felt easier to hide in plain sight. These patterns didn't begin because I wanted to rebel. They were extensions of a deeper truth: my body didn't feel like a safe place to be. Numbing was the only way I knew how to stay.

Self-harm is often misunderstood. Many people see it as dramatic, reckless, or done for attention. What they don't see is that it is often a way to survive.

Sometimes pain is the only thing that breaks through the numbness. Sometimes it is the only way to feel real again. Other times, it is a way to stop feeling anything at all.

The reasons can look different from the outside, but they often come from the same place. A body that has never known peace. A nervous system that is trying, in the only way it knows how, to cope with overwhelming pain.

Anyone who has lived through this deserves to hear the truth. You were never broken. You were in pain. You were coping the best you could with the tools you had. You needed comfort, not correction. You needed safety, not shame. What you carried was never yours to carry alone.

Reconnecting with a body that has held this kind of pain takes time. It cannot be rushed. It begins with gentleness and grows through consistency. This process might include therapy, trauma-informed healing, or sacred practices that slowly rebuild trust. There is no perfect way to return. There is only the choice to stop abandoning yourself.

When the body has been unsafe for years, embodiment must be approached like a sacred conversation—not a demand. Healing comes one breath at a time. It comes through tiny moments of softness where pain used to live. It comes through presence that doesn't push, and through listening that doesn't judge.

This is how we begin to come home again.

Coming Home — Daily Rituals for Reconnection

Coming back to your body is not a single moment. It's a return that happens again and again. Some days, it feels like peace. Other days, it feels like resistance. The journey isn't about fixing what's broken. It's about learning to stay present with what lives here now.

For a long time, I believed that embodiment meant feeling good all the time. I thought if I healed enough, I would wake up with calm breath, relaxed muscles, and unwavering confidence. What I've come to understand is that embodiment isn't about comfort. It's about honesty. The body doesn't promise ease—it promises truth.

Some days, that truth whispers. Other days, it roars. Both are valid.

To stay in a relationship with your body, you need rituals that are gentle, consistent, and attuned to your own rhythm. These practices don't have to be long or elaborate. In fact, the simpler they are, the more likely they are to become part of your daily life.

Here are some of the practices I return to again and again. Each one is a doorway home.

- Touch with intention. Place your hand on your heart, your belly, or your cheek. Feel the warmth of your own skin. Breathe into the places that usually tighten.

- Movement without performance. Let your body stretch, sway, or shake without needing it to look a certain way. Move for sensation, not appearance.
- Anchor with scent. Light a candle, apply essential oils, or breathe in something familiar. Scent travels straight to the emotional centers of the brain and can create an immediate sense of safety.
- Eat something slowly. Choose a food that feels nourishing. Notice its texture, temperature, and flavor. Let yourself be present with it, not distracted or rushed.
- Use water as medicine. Take a warm shower and imagine everything that doesn't belong to you washing away. Submerge your hands in cold water if you feel overwhelmed. Let water carry the weight for a moment.
- Name what you feel without fixing it. Try saying: "My chest feels tight. My jaw is clenched. My stomach is turning." Let the truth of your sensations exist without forcing them to change.
- Make a safe space for your body to rest. Create a corner with soft textures, dim lighting, and calming music or silence. Let it be a place where your nervous system knows it can settle.

These rituals are not requirements. They are invitations. Some days, you might only have the energy for one breath with your hand on your heart. That is enough. You don't have to do it all to be embodied. You only have to begin again, as often as it takes.

The body is not just a place of pain. It is also a place of wisdom, memory, and resilience. Every heartbeat, every shiver, every breath you take is proof that you are still here. That matters. Coming home to yourself is not a destination. It is a sacred, ongoing reunion.

Shadow Sheet

Reflective Questions — The Embodied Self

1. What messages did you receive about your body growing up? Were you taught to trust it, fear it, ignore it, or control it?

   ----

2. When do you feel most disconnected from your body? What emotions, memories, or situations tend to trigger that disconnection?

   ----

3. Can you recall a time when your body tried to communicate something to you—and you didn't feel safe enough to listen?

   ----

4. What survival strategies have you used to avoid sensation or emotion? (Examples might include self-harm, overworking, dissociation, perfectionism, numbing behaviors.)

----

5. Do you remember the first time you felt shame or confusion about something your body did or needed?

----

6. In what ways have you tried to protect yourself from your own body—or from what it holds?

----

7. What does the freeze response look like for you personally? How does it show up in your physical body or daily life?

----

8. What has helped you feel even a small sense of safety inside your body—past or present?

---

9. Which sensations do you find easiest to feel? Which ones do you avoid or find overwhelming?

---

10. How would it feel to treat your body as an ally instead of an enemy, even if just for one moment?

---

11. What daily ritual or sensory practice could help you begin building a more trusting relationship with your body?

---

12. If your body could speak freely today—without fear of being judged, punished, or silenced—what would it say?

About The Author

Emily Elizabeth Hickman is a behavioral health therapist, writer, and transformational guide born and raised in the Appalachian Mountains of eastern Kentucky, where she continues to live today. Her work is shaped by both professional training and lived experience, with a focus on helping individuals understand their emotional patterns, navigate life transitions, and move toward healing and self-discovery.

Emily holds a Master's degree in Mental Health Counseling and brings a background in coaching, leadership, and human services to her work. She is particularly passionate about exploring how early experiences, family dynamics, and attachment patterns influence identity, relationships, and personal growth. Her approach blends clinical insight with compassionate, relatable guidance grounded in real-life experience.

As a mother of two, a daughter and a son, Emily's perspective is also shaped by her commitment to generational healing and the desire to better understand how our past influences the way we love, connect, and show up in the world.

In addition to her nonfiction writing, Emily also writes poetry under the name Ember Evanesco Elderflower, where she explores themes of healing, identity, grief, and transformation. Her poetry reflects the emotional undercurrents behind the work she explores in her writing and professional practice.

The Daughter I Had to Be is her first book. She is currently working on her second book, The Space Between Replies, which explores attachment styles and the emotional dynamics that shape relationships.

Emily continues to live and work in the Appalachian Mountains, where she supports others in understanding themselves more deeply and creating meaningful, lasting change in their lives.